"*Game Changer 100* is more than just a book—it's a powerful guide to unlocking your true potential. The insights are straightforward, yet deeply impactful, providing a clear guide to transform your life. Prepare to be inspired, empowered, and motivated to step into the life God has planned for you."

—**Dr. Mary Drabik**
President, South Florida Bible College and Theological Seminary

"I have known Pastor Steve Gowdy for years, and he has a true heart for seeing people come to salvation and grow deeper in their walk with the Lord. The resource before you is designed to do just that. It is filled with eternal truths that God can use in your life if you trust Him. The timeless principles in this book will deepen your understanding of who God is and who you are in Christ. As you read it and interact with the text be prepared to be blessed, challenged, and transformed by the majesty of our Lord and His desire to use you for His glory. Additionally, Pastor Gowdy has included a valuable guide on how to lead someone to a saving knowledge of our Lord Jesus Christ."

—**Robert E. Nix, PhD**
President, Berean Bible Institute

As a longtime friend and admirer of Steve Gowdy's contagious, fun spirit, it has always been obvious that his optimism comes from his unapologetic, strong belief in the truths of God's Word—who he is in Christ and what God has done in his life!

I've watched Steve and his wife, Darlene, navigate great obstacles with unwavering resolve, rooted in their faith in what God has done and will continue to do. This book flows from what Steve believes and desires for others to recognize—the incredible work of God in the life of every believer. I have long appreciated the work of the late Lewis Sperry Chafer in his *Systematic Theology* (published in 1948), where, in Volume III, beginning on page 235, he carefully explains the 33 miraculous works of God carried out instantaneously at the moment of salvation. The gift of salvation for undeserving man is truly a *Game Changer*—both in this life and for eternity. Thank you, Steve, for drawing our attention back to these foundational truths through your book. May it encourage many others!"

—**Ken B. Kemper, PhD**
President, Grace Christian University

"Have you ever said, 'Poor me?' If so—or even if you've never spoken those words—read and reread *Game Changer 100*. In it, you'll discover the incredible riches God lavished upon you the moment you believed in the Lord Jesus as your Savior. You are truly RICH!"

—Dr. Samuel Vinton, Jr.
President Emeritus – Grace Christian University
Executive Director Emeritus – Grace Ministries International

"My relationship with Steve Gowdy began over 40 years ago when we were college roommates. We have maintained a friendship that has spanned more than four decades. To this day, I continue to be encouraged by how God uses Steve to promote the Gospel and guide others as they grow in their faith. *Game Changer 100* is a book that teaches foundational truths of Scripture while providing practical insights for Christians to grow in their spiritual journey."

—Dr. Bill Doran
Retired CEO and Principal, Illinois Public School System

"If you're looking for a single resource, a quick where to find it guide that answers the many needs of our heart as we grow in Christ, this is it! Steve has taken a full library of resources and combined them in to one valuable resource. It is like a superfood, multi-vitamin for the Christian life in one book."

—Dennis W. Smith
Pastor, Valley Bible Church

"I've read *Game Changer 100 Truths* by Stephen Gowdy, and I'm truly impressed. This book with study guide questions is a powerful tool to help us understand our position in Christ. I'm fully behind this project and look forward to using it as a study guide with the men I'm mentoring. Stephen, thank you for being obedient to our Lord in bringing this resource to life. Your brother in Christ."

—Dave Kepner
Executive Director, New Creations Recovery

"Marvelous things happen when we accept Jesus Christ as Lord and Savior, including becoming children of God and being delivered from darkness into His kingdom. In *Game Changer 100*, Steve has carefully arranged powerful truths from Scripture that renew our minds and help us live a Godly life. This book is both instructional and encouraging, offering a clear pathway for believers to grow in the grace and knowledge of our Lord Jesus Christ."

—David Albrecht
International Media Minister

"Satan does not want you to discover the full riches of God's grace and the countless gifts He has given to those who believe. In this book, Steve has masterfully gathered these treasures into one place, offering you a clear and uplifting guide to understanding and embracing all that God has provided. A must-read for every believer seeking to walk in the fullness of their faith."

—**Steve Postma**
Church Elder and Bible Teacher

"This book is timely. I was looking for a devotional resource to use with my 13 year old son as we begin a 'rite of passage' process for him this year. I will be connecting with him for weekly devotions, and this offers a succinct guide for meaningful/foundational discussions of faith."

—**Zak Sorensen**
A Sinner Saved by Grace (the Author of this book thinks Zak is a Marketing Genius)

"*Game Changer 100* is a thoughtfully crafted guide offering practical insights and key biblical principles to nurture spiritual growth, deepen understanding, and fortify your faith. It provides a solid framework for reflection and personal development, inspiring readers to apply timeless truths in their daily lives."

—**Tim Postma, Sr.**
Cybersecurity Engineer

"Author Steve Gowdy has dedicated most of his adult life discovering and sharing new ways for believers at every stage of life to grow spiritually and deepen their biblical knowledge. *Game Changer 100* is yet another powerful resource to help readers understand the transformative power of the gospel and their identity as a new creation in Christ.

Steve, like me, understands that the Christian life isn't always the easiest life, but it's undoubtedly the BEST life. His authenticity and relatability make this resource truly special!"

—**Pastor Troy Sergey**
Grace Church, Indianapolis, Indiana

"*Game Changer 100* is a wonderful encouragement and a lovely reminder of 'every spiritual blessing' given to us by God, whether we are new believers or have been on this journey for a while. God's truth is immutable and available to us wherever we are at on that path."

—**John Kelly**
Engineer, STEM Educator, and Friend

"*Game Changer 100* is an incredible book to use for every believer. It has a beautiful way of blending deep, foundational, profound truths with a practical and applicable style. From the person who just received Christ to those who've been walking alongside Him for years—this book is for you. As you work though this book, you'll find yourself pondering God's goodness and at times throwing your hands to the heavens and thanking The Father for the Gift of Jesus.

The truths found in this book made my heart soar as I read all the ways that my life is different because of what was done for me through God's love, Jesus' sacrifice and the Holy Sprits indwelling. Thank you Steve for writing this amazing book."

—**Scott Albers**
Pastor, Evangelist, Transportation Executive

"*Game Changer: 100 Truths That Transform Your Life the Moment You Believe* is an inspirational and profound journey through the transformative power of faith in Jesus Christ. This book is a treasure trove of biblical truths designed to unlock God's plan and elevate believers to a life filled with divine purpose and grace.

Game Changer 100 is a must-read for anyone seeking to deepen their faith and understand the profound changes that occur the moment they believe in Jesus Christ. The book's structure, with its 100 short, easy-to-read articles, makes it accessible and engaging for both new believers and seasoned Christians. Each truth serves as a 'Grace Power-Up,' recharging the spirit and shedding light on life's complexities.

Game Changer 100 is more than just a book; it's a journey that will challenge, uplift, and reveal the infinite possibilities of a life lived for Christ. I highly recommend it to anyone looking to unlock God's plan and level up to a life of purpose."

—**Pastor Dwight Anderson**
Senior Pastor, Bethesda Chruch, Executive Director, Prison Mission Association

"Steve has been a source of great encouragement to us—in life and ministry. This book is meant to be a source of encouragement for each reader regardless where he/she is in his/her walk with the Lord. We can feel Steve's love for the Lord and for you, the reader. His words of encouragement are clear and heartfelt. As you journey with him through this book, you too will experience the truths of God's Word, which are sure to impact your life, strengthen your spiritual growth, and enrich your ministry. Enjoy this dive into these important truths."

—**Dave and Linda Holton**
Pastor

"Whether you've known Jesus Christ for many years or have just recently come to know Him, Steve Gowdy's book *Game Changer 100 Truths* is a must read! If you are a veteran Christian, these 100 Truths are sure to reawaken awe and wonder for what Christ has done in you. And if you are new to the Faith, then let these 100 Truths wash over you, refresh you, and solidify your trust and love for Christ. 'Therefore, if anyone is in Christ, the new creation has come: The old has gone, the new is here!'" – 2 Corinthians 5:17 (NIV)

—**Rob Fisher**
Pastor, Author

Game Changer

100 TRUTHS THAT TRANSFORM YOUR LIFE THE MOMENT YOU BELIEVE

STEPHEN C. GOWDY

BRIGHT IDEAS PUBLISHING

Green Valley | Arizona | USA

WRITING THIS BOOK BROUGHT ME TO TEARS. THINKING ABOUT WHAT THE LORD HAS DONE FOR ME ON THE CROSS AND WHAT I RECEIVED AT THE MOMENT OF SALVATION, MY HEART OVERFLOWS WITH JOY.

—STEPHEN C. GOWDY

Stephen C. Gowdy is a registered Literary Artist with the Choctaw Nation of Oklahoma. As an American Indian author, his work is inspired by faith, heritage, and a commitment to sharing transformative truths based upon God's Word.

Game Changer

100 TRUTHS THAT TRANSFORM YOUR LIFE THE MOMENT YOU BELIEVE

STEPHEN C. GOWDY

BRIGHT IDEAS PUBLISHING

Green Valley | Arizona | USA

Copyright © 2025 By Stephen C. Gowdy

Game Changer: 100 Truths That Transform Your Life the Moment You Believe
      Edition 1.1a
Printed in the USA.

Published by BRIGHT IDEAS PUBLISHING
1352 N Paseo Maravilloso
Green Valley, Arizona 85614
United States of America
www.BrightIdeasPublishing.com

ALL RIGHTS RESERVED
ISBN-13: 978-1-7375276-4-0

Library of Congress Control Number: 2025900362

NIV (New International Version®) Scripture quotations taken from The Holy Bible, New International Version® NIV® Copyright © 1973, 1978, 1984, 2011 by Biblica, Inc. Used with permission. All rights reserved worldwide.

RSV (Revised Standard Version): Scripture quotations are from the Revised Standard Version of the Bible (RSV), Copyright ©1946, 1952, 1971, 1973 by the Division of Christian Education of the National Council of the Churches of Christ in the United States of America. Used by permission. All rights reserved.

NASB (New American Standard Bible): Scripture quotations are taken from the New American Standard Bible® (NASB), Copyright ©1960, 1962, 1963, 1968, 1971, 1972, 1973, 1975, 1977, 1995, 2020 by The Lockman Foundation. Used by permission. All rights reserved.

THIS PUBLICATION IS PROTECTED UNDER FEDERAL COPYRIGHT LAWS. REPRODUCTION OR DISTRIBUTION OF THIS OR ANY OTHER PUBLICATION, INCLUDING PUBLICATIONS, ILLUSTRATIONS AND EDITIONS WHICH ARE OUT OF PRINT, IS PROHIBITED UNLESS SPECIFICALLY AUTHORIZED IN WRITING. THIS INCLUDES, BUT IS NOT LIMITED TO, ANY FORM OF REPRODUCTION OR DISTRIBUTION ON OR THROUGH THE INTERNET, INCLUDING POSTING, SCANNING, OR EMAIL TRANSMISSION.

For bulk purchases for a church or Bible study group, information, questions, or to request written permissions for use, please contact: contact@BrightIdeasPublishing.com

Author Picture Courtesy of Tutku Tours May 17, 2022 in Petra, Jordon
Cover design by Jason Christenson

To my Savior, Jesus Christ, whose love, sacrifice, and grace have made all things new in my life. Every word in this book is a testimony to Your faithfulness. You, Lord, are faithful and worthy to be trusted in every situation, big and small. You are worthy.

To those who are seeking, doubting, or just beginning their walk with Christ—this is for you. May these truths open your eyes to the boundless love of God and the incredible transformations that await.

—Stephen C. Gowdy

Foreword

As someone passionate about encouraging families to embrace the transformative love of Jesus Christ, I am honored to introduce *Game Changer: 100 Truths That Transform Your Life the Moment You Believe*.

Stephen C. Gowdy's words are a powerful reminder of the life-changing truths we receive when we place our faith in Christ.

THIS BOOK ISN'T JUST A COLLECTION OF INSIGHTS—IT'S A ROADMAP FOR BELIEVERS OF ALL AGES TO DISCOVER THEIR IDENTITY IN CHRIST AND WALK CONFIDENTLY IN FREEDOM.

This book isn't just a collection of insights—it's a roadmap for believers of all ages to discover their identity in Christ and walk confidently in freedom. Each biblical truth Stephen shares deepens our understanding of life's purpose and inspires gratitude in our hearts.

What stands out to me is how these truths equip us to pass on a legacy of faith to the next generation. By living out these truths, we inspire our children and leave behind a Christ-centered heritage.

It's my hope that *Game Changer 100* will inspire and transform your life, drawing you closer to God and equipping you to stand firm in Christ and live boldly for Him.

Blessings,
Kevin Sorbo

> Kevin Sorbo is a distinguished American actor, producer, and director, with over 90 film and television projects, and over 100 million viewers impacted globally. Kevin was renowned for his iconic role as Hercules in *Hercules: The Legendary Journeys*. It ran for six seasons, it became one of the highest-rated syndicated television shows in the world at that time. Kevin champions Christian values and family unity. His works, including *God's Not Dead* & *Let There Be Light*, and one of the authors favorites *Soul Surfer* demonstrates that movies reflecting traditional values can achieve significant box office success, inspiring and uplifting audiences around the world.

Prologue

The moment we believe—truly believe—is a moment that changes everything. It's not just an act of faith; it's the genesis of transformation, the first step to a life of divine purpose. In that split second when we receive God's free gift of salvation, something extraordinary happens: He welcomes us into His Forever Family. Our identity is rewritten, our future redefined, and our hearts renewed.

THE MOMENT WE BELIEVE—TRULY BELIEVE—IS A MOMENT THAT CHANGES EVERYTHING.

This book, *Game Changer: 100 Truths That Transform Your Life the Moment You Believe*, was born out of a deep desire to share these profound truths with you. Whether you are new in your faith or have walked with Christ for years, these truths are timeless. They testify to the miracles of salvation—some we can understand, others are mysteries beyond comprehension. Yet all point to the undeniable reality of a God who loves us more deeply than we can imagine.

IT IS MY PRAYER THAT THESE TRUTHS INSPIRE YOU, ENCOURAGE YOU, AND REMIND YOU OF THE LIMITLESS GRACE AND POWER OF OUR SAVIOR.

Through these pages, I hope to illuminate the incredible changes that occur the moment we say *yes* to Jesus. It is my prayer that these truths inspire you, encourage you, and remind you of the limitless grace and power of our Savior. May they transform the way you live, love, and pursue the purpose God has designed uniquely for you.

Welcome to a journey that will challenge you, uplift you, and above all, reveal the infinite possibilities of a life lived for Christ.

Table of Contents

Words of Encouragement	i
Dedication	xi
Foreword By Kevin Sorbo	xii
Prologue	xiii
Table of Contents	14
Introduction	18
How to Read and Understand This Book	19

Foundational Truths   21

1. You Are Transformed from Death to Life	22
2. Your Name Is Written in the Book of Life	24
3. You Are Bought with a Great Price	26
4. You Are Made Perfect in Christ	30
5. You Are Justified by Faith	32

The Believer's New Identity   35

6. You Are Adopted as Sons	36
7. You Are Chosen to Be Part of God's Family	38
8. You Can Call God Abba Father	40
9. You Are a Citizen of Heaven	42
10. You Are Called a Saint	44

The Work of Christ   47

11. You Are Redeemed by Christ's Blood	48
12. Your Sins Are Forgiven	50
13. Your Sins Are Fully Atoned	52
14. Christ Paid the Penalty for Your Sin	54
15. You Are Given a Crown of Righteousness	56

The Role of the Holy Spirit   59

16. You Are Baptized into the Body by the Holy Spirit	60
17. You Are Indwelt by the Holy Spirit	62
18. You Are Sanctified by the Spirit	64
19. You Have the Power to Love Fully	66
20. You Are Sealed by the Holy Spirit	68

Living Out Your Faith   71

21. You Have Peace with God	72
22. You Are Given Armor from God to Defend Yourself	74
23. You Walk as a Child of Light	76
24. You Can Find Contentment through God's Grace	78
25. You Are Free from the Burden of Self-Righteousness	80

God's Grace and Sovereignty   83

26. You Are Eternally Secure in Christ   84
27. You Are Looking for the Blessed Hope and Glorious Appearing   86
28. You Are Predestined in Christ   88
29. You Are Fully Accepted by God   90
30. You Are Reconciled to God   92

The Believer's Privileges   95

31. You Are Added to the Body of Believers   96
32. You Are Heavenly Associated with God's Creation   98
33. You Are Anointed and Empowered by God   100
34. You Are Given the Title of Ambassador   102
35. You Are Part of God's Family and Household   104

The Believer's Future Hope   107

36. Your Future with Christ Is Guaranteed   108
37. You Are Promised an Eternal Inheritance   110
38. You Are Spiritually Glorified and Await Full Glorification   112
39. You Were Given the Gift of God—Eternal Life   114
40. Your Conscience Is Cleansed by Christ   116

Living for God's Glory   119

41. You Can Boast in Christ Alone   120
42. You Are Redeemed by God   122
43. You Are Buried with Christ   124
44. You Are Saved by Grace   126
45. You Are Positioned in Christ   128

Empowered by the Spirit   131

46. You Are Victorious over Darkness   132
47. You Are Blessed with Every Spiritual Blessing   134
48. You Are Complete in Christ   136
49. You Have Empowered Living through Christ   138
50. You Are Delivered from the Power of Darkness   140

Practical Faith   143

51. You Have a Heavenly Calling   144
52. You Are Judged as Righteous, Moving from Guilt to Glory   146
53. You Are Taught by God's Grace   148
54. You Are Given the Fruit of the Spirit   150
55. You Will Be Rewarded for Labor in God's Service   152

Unity and Service in the Body of Christ   155

56. You Have the Privilege to Run Life's Race with Christ   156
57. You Are Rewarded for Diligently Seeking God   158
58. You Can Trust in God Rather than Human Wisdom   160
59. You Are Called to Be Known for Your Faith   162

60. You Have Spiritual Fathers and Leaders to Imitate	164

God's Grace and Provision — 167

61. You Welcome the Good News with Joy	168
62. You Are Partakers of Christ	170
63. You Are Honored to Serve and Suffer for the Gospel	172
64. You Can Be Confident that God Will Finish His Work in You	174
65. You Have Full Access to God	176

The Mysteries of God Revealed — 179

66. You Find Grace and Mercy in Time of Need	180
67. You Are Part of the Mystery of the Body of Christ	182
68. You Have a Guaranteed Formula for Joy	184
69. You Are a Member of the Church (Jews and Gentiles Together)	186
70. You Are Given the Body of Christ as an Example for Marriage	188

The Believer's Strength in Christ — 191

71. You Can Approach God with Freedom and Confidence	192
72. You Can Now Stand Firm in Christ	194
73. You Experience Diversity and Unity in the Body of Christ	196
74. You Can Embrace Weakness for God's Glory	198
75. You Are Delivered from the Law	200

The Believer's Role and Responsibilities — 203

76. You Have Supernatural Power for Relationships	204
77. You Win Spiritual Battles on Your Knees	208
78. You Can Trust God's Sovereignty over Revenge	210
79. You Are Entrusted with the Message of Reconciliation	212
80. You Are Made Alive to Worship and Serve	214

Living a Transformed Life — 217

81. You Have Freedom through Prayer	218
82. You Are Called to a Heavenly Mindset	220
83. You Can Depend on God Completely	222
84. You Are Comforted by the God of All Comfort	224
85. You Are Free to Forgive	226

Eternity and Assurance — 229

86. You Can Cultivate an Un-offendable Heart	230
87. You Are Equipped with the Power of God's Word	232
88. You Are Dead to the Law	234
89. You Have Christ as Your Foundation	236
90. You Are God's Temple	238

Power and Authority in Christ — 241

91. You Have God's Undeserved Gift of Love	242
92. You Are Given an Advocate	244
93. You Are a Co-Laborer with Christ	246

94. Your Life is a Letter Written from Heaven	248
95. You Are More than a Conqueror	250

The Believer's Testimony to the World — **253**

96. You Are Entrusted with a Simple Gospel to Share	254
97. You Are Given the Gift of Repentance	256
98. You Are a New Creation in Christ	258
99. You Are Brought Near to God	260
100. You Are Given by the Father to the Son as a Love Gift	262

How to Share Truths with Others — **265**

Romans Roadway for Salvation	266
Become an Ambassador in 60 Seconds	268

References, Resources, & Further Reading — **273**

Scriptures Referenced	274
Resources	275
Special Thanks	276
Author's Note	279
Why "Game Changer?"	281
A Personal Reflection	282
References (Sorted by Theologian)	283
About the Author	288
Before You Go	290

Introduction

What if you could uncover 100 truths that have the power to change your life forever? Truths that lead you toward spiritual growth and reveal the boundless love of our Heavenly Father to your heart. Imagine discovering 100 reasons to embrace His blessings. These blessings go far beyond anything you could ask, think, or imagine.

This book is more than just a collection of thoughts; it's a journey—one that takes you through 100 short, easy-to-read articles designed to transform your spiritual perspective and deepen your faith. Each of these truths serves as a "Grace Power-Up", a burst of divine insight that recharges your spirit and sheds light on life's complexities. Think of them as puzzle pieces in the grand, God-crafted design of your life. As each piece finds its place, your understanding expands, your faith grows, and you feel drawn closer to the profound truth of God's perfect plan.

"These 100 truths are here to bring you peace in chaos, comfort when you feel weary, encouragement when you face uncertainty, and freedom from anything that holds you back."

I've never been much of a fan of puzzling, though my wife and 92-year-old mom love it. Sometimes I'm gently encouraged (or maybe strongly persuaded) to join in on a family project. And while it's not my first choice of activity, before long, I'm celebrating every piece that clicks into place. Often, it's not the final piece but a challenging one that completes a section and suddenly brings the whole picture into focus. Life is like that—each truth we uncover helps us see God's design more clearly, and every step forward deserves its own celebration. If life were a melody, these truths might also be "Grace Notes," each adding beauty and harmony to the song of your journey.

They reflect God's unchanging love, His purpose for your life, and His desire for you to walk in His abundant blessings. Through these pages, you'll begin to see the world through the lens of faith, hope, and grace.

Whether you're a new believer, someone longing for a deeper relationship with Christ, or simply in need of a reminder of God's promises, this book is for you. Dive in and discover how these truths can transform your life and help you walk boldly into the amazing future God has planned for you.

How to Read and Understand This Book

This book is a heartfelt resource designed to support your growth, understanding, and encouragement in your faith journey. It is my prayer that each of the 100 articles helps you explore God's truths and their significance in your daily life. Each article follows a consistent and intentional layout to guide you as you draw closer to Him:

Title and Focus: Each article begins with a key truth, such as "You are Justified by Faith," which serves as the foundation for the concept being explored.

Scriptural Reference: A Bible verse is the best place to start and anchors the truth in God's Word, like Romans 5:1: "Therefore, since we have been justified through faith, we have peace with God through our Lord Jesus Christ." (NIV)

Highlights:

- **Transformational Truth**: Explains the significance of the truth. For example, "At the moment of salvation, you are declared righteous by faith in Christ."
- **Foundational Word**: Unpacks the meaning of key biblical terms, such as "Justified" (*Greek: dikaioo*), meaning to be acquitted or declared righteous.
- **Theological Insight**: Shares wisdom from theologians or Christian leaders, such as Martin Luther's famous statement: "Justification is the chief article from which all other doctrines flow."[1]

Grace Power-Up Application and a Reflective Prayer: Encourages you to prayerfully consider questions like:

- What does this truth reveal while Examining God's Character?
- How can this truth bring peace or encouragement in your life?
- How can you live out this truth in your daily walk?

The desire is to humbly share these thoughts with deep gratitude for the grace God has shown in my life. My hope and prayer are that, as you reflect and meditate on these profound truths, you will see God's love and purpose for your life in new and meaningful ways. May each article draw you closer to our Heavenly Father and inspire a deeper, more intimate relationship with Him.

---

[1] Martin Luther, *Commentary on Galatians* (Grand Rapids: Kregel Publications, 1979), p. 20.

1. You Are Transformed from Death to Life

Scripture

Ephesians 2:4–5 "But because of his great love for us, God, who is rich in mercy, made us alive with Christ even when we were dead in transgressions—it is by grace you have been saved." (NIV)

Highlights

- **Transformational Truth:** At the moment of salvation, by God's mercy you are brought from spiritual death to life, receiving the promise of eternal life through faith in Jesus Christ.

- **Foundational Word:** "Mercy" (Greek: eleos) signifies God's compassion and kindness, extended to humanity by withholding deserved punishment and providing new life and salvation through Jesus Christ.

- **Theological Insight:** Timothy Keller shares, "Through the person and work of Jesus Christ, our spiritual deadness is overcome, and we are brought into newness of life."[2]

Grace Power-Up: You Are Transformed from Death to Life

QUESTION 1: EXAMINING GOD'S CHARACTER

Where do you think you would be if God had **not** provided a way to move from Death to Life, leaving you in spiritual death? How would that make you feel?

---

[2] Keller, Timothy. *Encounters with Jesus: Unexpected Answers to Life's Biggest Questions*. Dutton, 2013, p. 102.

QUESTION 2: CURRENT CIRCUMSTANCES

How does the promise of eternal life give you hope and perspective during moments of fear, doubt, or uncertainty?

___

___

___

QUESTION 3: FUTURE PLANS - KNOWING THIS TRUTH

How can you live in a way that reflects the joy and gratitude of being brought from death to life in Christ?

___

___

___

A Prayer of Gratitude for Eternal Life

Heavenly Father,

Thank You for bringing me from spiritual death to life through Your mercy and grace. I am in awe of Your love and the promise of eternal life You have given me. Help me to live each day in the joy and confidence of this truth.

Teach me to trust in You fully, especially in times of fear or doubt, and to share the hope of eternal life with others. May my life be a reflection of Your saving grace and a testimony to Your great love.

In Jesus's Name,
Amen.

2. Your Name Is Written in the Book of Life

Scripture

Philippians 4:3 "Yes, and I ask you, my true companion, help these women since they have contended at my side in the cause of the gospel, along with Clement and the rest of my co-workers, whose names are in the book of life." (NIV)

Revelation 13:8 "All inhabitants of the earth will worship the beast—all whose names have not been written in the Lamb's book of life, the Lamb who was slain from the creation of the world." (NIV)

Revelation 20:15 "Anyone whose name was not found written in the book of life was thrown into the lake of fire." (NIV)

Revelation 21:27 "Nothing impure will ever enter it, nor will anyone who does what is shameful or deceitful, but only those whose names are written in the Lamb's book of life." (NIV)

Highlights

- **Transformational Truth:** At the moment of salvation, your name is permanently inscribed in the Book of Life, symbolizing your eternal security in Christ.
- **Foundational Word:** "Written" (Greek: *grapho*) means to record or engrave, indicating a lasting and unchangeable record.
- **Theological Insight**: John Gill states, "This book contains the names of all who are chosen and redeemed by Christ."[3]

Grace Power-Up: God Has Written Your Name in the Book of Life

QUESTION 1: EXAMINING GOD'S CHARACTER

---

[3] John Gill, *Exposition of the Old and New Testaments*, commentary on Revelation 13:8.

How would your sense of security and hope be affected if God had **not** permanently inscribed your name in the Book of Life?

_____

_____

QUESTION 2: CURRENT CIRCUMSTANCES

How does knowing your name is written in the Book of Life give you confidence and assurance when facing doubts or fears about your salvation?

_____

_____

QUESTION 3: FUTURE PLANS - KNOWING THIS TRUTH

How can the certainty of your name in the Book of Life inspire you to live boldly and share the gospel with others?

_____

_____

A Prayer of Gratitude for Your Name Being Written in the Book of Life

Heavenly Father,

Thank You for writing my name in the Lamb's Book of Life. I am humbled and overjoyed by the assurance of eternal security through Christ. Help me to live in the confidence of this truth, free from fear and full of hope.

Teach me to honor this privilege by living boldly for You, sharing the good news of salvation with others. May my life glorify You and reflect the joy of knowing I belong to You forever.

In Jesus's Name, Amen.

3. You Are Bought with a Great Price

Scripture

1 Corinthians 6:20 "You were bought at a price. Therefore honor God with your bodies." (NIV)

1 Corinthians 7:23 "You were bought at a price; do not become slaves of human beings." (NIV)

Romans 3:24–25 "And all are justified freely by his grace through the redemption that came by Christ Jesus. God presented Christ as a sacrifice of atonement, through the shedding of his blood—to be received by faith." (NIV)

Hebrews 2:17 "For this reason he had to be made like them, fully human in every way, in order that he might become a merciful and faithful high priest in service to God, and that he might make atonement for the sins of the people." (NIV)

1 John 2:2 "He is the atoning sacrifice for our sins, and not only for ours but also for the sins of the whole world." (NIV)

Highlights

- **Transformational Truth:** At the moment of salvation, when you accept God's free gift and become a believer in Christ, Christ's payment for all your sins is applied in full. His perfect life, offered as a sacrifice, removes every barrier that once separated you from God and opens the way to eternal life in heaven.

- **Foundational Words:** "Bought" (Greek: *agorazō*) means to purchase or redeem, emphasizing that believers were bought with a price, Christ's sacrificial death. "Propitiation" (Greek: *hilastērion*) refers to Christ's atoning sacrifice that satisfies God's wrath against sin, restoring believers to favor with God.

- **Theological Insight:** Dr. Sam Vinton, Jr. shares, "The blood of Christ is precious and infinite in value, for it was the only price that could fully pay for the sin of humanity and bring reconciliation to God."[4]

---

[4] Sam Vinton, Jr., *The Precious Blood: Redemption and Reconciliation Through Christ* (Grand Rapids, MI: Grace Publications, 2006), p. 88.

Grace Power-Up: God Bought You at a Great Price

QUESTION 1: EXAMINING GOD'S CHARACTER

How would your view of God's love and justice change if Christ had **not** paid the full price for your sins, leaving you unable to approach Him or enter heaven?

_____

_____

_____

QUESTION 2: CURRENT CIRCUMSTANCES

How does understanding that you were bought at a great price inspire you to live a life that honors God in your actions, thoughts, and choices?

_____

_____

_____

QUESTION 3: FUTURE PLANS - KNOWING THIS TRUTH

How can you share the message of Christ's sacrificial payment with others, demonstrating gratitude for the price He paid for your redemption?

_____

_____

_____

A Prayer of Gratitude for Being Bought at a Great Price

Heavenly Father,

Thank You for the priceless gift of Christ's sacrifice, which paid in full the penalty for my sins and removed every barrier between me and You. I am humbled and grateful for the infinite value of His blood, which has redeemed me and reconciled me to You, I receive this gift of Eternal Life. Thank You.

Help me to live a life that reflects the magnitude of this sacrifice, honoring You in every area of my life. Teach me to share this truth with others, pointing them to the hope and salvation found in Christ alone.

In Jesus's Name, Amen.

REVIEW

After reading the first few transformational truths, what was most impactful?

_____

_____

_____

_____

_____

_____

_____

_____

_____

_____

4. You Are Made Perfect in Christ

Scripture

Colossians 1:22 "But now he has reconciled you by Christ's physical body through death to present you holy in his sight, without blemish and free from accusation." (NIV)

Hebrews 10:14 "For by one sacrifice he has made perfect forever those who are being made holy." (NIV)

Highlights

- **Transformational Truth:** At the moment of salvation, you are viewed by God as perfect and blameless through the righteousness of Christ, a standing that is complete yet will be fully realized in eternity.

- **Foundational Word:** "Perfect" (Greek: *teleioō*) means complete, mature, or without blemish.

- **Theological Insight**: John Calvin states, "In Christ, the believer is declared perfect, not by their own merit, but through the imputed righteousness of Christ, which fulfills all the demands of God's holiness."[5]

Grace Power-Up: Seen as Perfect in Christ

QUESTION 1: EXAMINING GOD'S CHARACTER

How would your relationship with God be affected if He did **not** view you as perfect in Christ, leaving you to stand before Him in your own flawed righteousness?

_____

_____

---

[5] John Calvin, *Institutes of the Christian Religion*, Book III, Chapter 11, Section 2 (Edinburgh: Calvin Translation Society, 1845).

QUESTION 2: CURRENT CIRCUMSTANCES

How does knowing that God sees you as perfect and blameless in Christ give you peace and confidence, especially when you struggle with guilt or feelings of inadequacy?

_____

_____

_____

QUESTION 3: FUTURE PLANS - KNOWING THIS TRUTH

How can you live with gratitude and purpose, reflecting the righteousness of Christ in your daily actions and relationships?

_____

_____

_____

A Prayer of Gratitude for Being Seen as Perfect in Christ

Heavenly Father,

Thank You for seeing me as perfect and blameless through the righteousness of Christ. I am humbled and grateful that I can stand before You, free from accusation, not because of my works, but because of His sacrifice. Help me to rest in this truth and let it shape my identity and confidence.

Teach me to live in gratitude and to reflect Christ's righteousness in all I do, pointing others to the hope and peace found in Him. May my life bring glory to You and honor the perfection I have been given in Christ.

In Jesus's Name,
Amen.

5. You Are Justified by Faith

Scripture

Romans 5:1 "Therefore, since we have been justified through faith, we have peace with God through our Lord Jesus Christ." (NIV)

Highlights

- **Transformational Truth:** At the moment of salvation, you are declared righteous by faith in Christ.
- **Foundational Word:** "Justified" (Greek: *dikaioo*) means to be acquitted or declared righteous.
- **Theological Insight:** Martin Luther: "Justification is the chief article from which all other doctrines flow."[6]

Grace Power-Up: Justification by Faith

QUESTION 1: EXAMINING GOD'S CHARACTER

Where would you stand before God if He had **not** provided a way for you to be declared righteous through faith in Christ?

_____

_____

_____

---

[6] Martin Luther, *Commentary on Galatians* (Grand Rapids: Kregel Publications, 1979), p. 20.

QUESTION 2: CURRENT CIRCUMSTANCES

How does knowing you are justified by faith bring peace and confidence when facing guilt or feelings of inadequacy?

_____

_____

_____

QUESTION 3: FUTURE PLANS - KNOWING THIS TRUTH

How can you live each day in the freedom and joy of being declared righteous by God, reflecting His grace to others?

_____

_____

_____

A Prayer of Gratitude for Justification by Faith

Heavenly Father,

Thank You for justifying me through faith in Christ. I am humbled by Your grace that declares me righteous, not because of anything I have done, but because of Jesus' sacrifice. Help me to live in the peace and assurance of this truth, resting in the freedom You provide.

Teach me to share this hope with others, reflecting Your love and grace in all that I do. May my life be a testimony to Your goodness and mercy.

In Jesus's Name,
Amen.

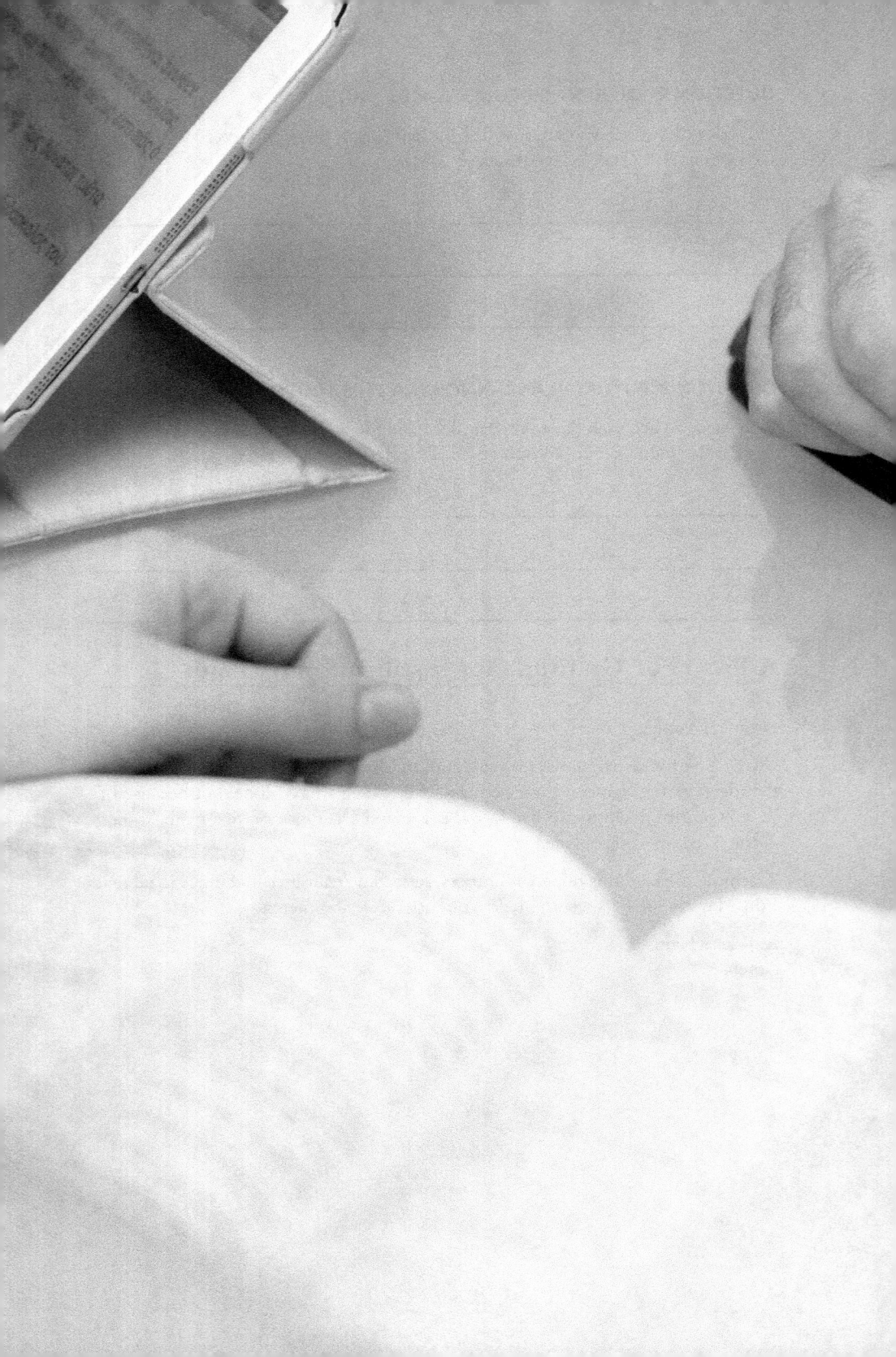

The Believer's New Identity

6. You Are Adopted as Sons

Scripture

Galatians 4:4–5 "But when the set time had fully come, God sent his Son, born of a woman, born under the law, to redeem those under the law, that we might receive adoption to sonship." (NIV)

Romans 8:23 "Not only so, but we ourselves, who have the firstfruits of the Spirit, groan inwardly as we wait eagerly for our adoption to sonship, the redemption of our bodies." (NIV)

Highlights

- **Transformational Truth:** At the moment of salvation, you are spiritually adopted to sonship and upon Christ's return will receive the full rights and privileges as His children. This adoption reflects God's grace and your new identity in Christ.

- **Foundational Word:** "Adoption" (Greek: *huiothesia*) signifies a legal act of making someone a son or daughter, granting them all the rights of family membership.

- **Theological Insight:** Aaron Menikoff says, "Adoption is the gracious act of God wherein He makes justified sinners His beloved children."[7]

Grace Power-Up: Adoption into God's Family

QUESTION 1: EXAMINING GOD'S CHARACTER

Where would you find yourself if God had **not** extended His grace, and you could no longer look forward to being adopted as sons, with all the rights of a son (or daughter)?

_____

_____

---

[7] Aaron Menikoff, (2019). *Adoption: The Heart of the Gospel. In Character Matters: Shepherding in the Fruit of the Spirit* (Wheaton, IL: Crossway.) p. 143.

QUESTION 2: CURRENT CIRCUMSTANCES

How does knowing you will be adopted into God's family help you face feelings of loneliness, rejection, or insecurity?

_____

_____

_____

QUESTION 3: FUTURE PLANS - KNOWING THIS TRUTH

How can you live out your identity knowing your future holds an adoption as Son's of God in your interactions with others this week?

_____

_____

_____

A Prayer of Gratitude for Anticipation for Adoption

Heavenly Father, thank You for adopting me into Your family through Jesus Christ. I am amazed at the love and grace that brought me from being lost to being adopted to sonship. Help me to live with confidence and joy in the knowledge of this privilege.

Teach me to reflect Your love to others, welcoming them as family in Christ. May my life bring honor to You and point others toward the joy of being Your child.

In Jesus's Name, Amen.

7. You Are Chosen to Be Part of God's Family

Scripture

1 Thessalonians 1:4 "For we know, brothers and sisters loved by God, that he has chosen you." (NIV)

Romans 8:33 "Who will bring any charge against those whom God has chosen? It is God who justifies." (NIV)

Colossians 3:12 "Therefore, as God's chosen people, holy and dearly loved, clothe yourselves with compassion, kindness, humility, gentleness and patience." (NIV)

Titus 1:1 "Paul, a servant of God and an apostle of Jesus Christ to further the faith of God's elect and their knowledge of the truth that leads to godliness." (NIV)

Highlights

- **Transformational Truth:** At the moment of salvation, you were chosen (elected) by God the Father to be part of the Body of Christ.
- **Foundational Word:** "Elected" (*Greek: eklektos*) means chosen or selected, indicating God's sovereign choice in salvation.
- **Theological Insight:** Charles Swindoll: "Election is a divine mystery, a gracious choice by God that brings believers into His family, assuring us of His love and purpose for our lives."[8]

Grace Power-Up: Elected to Be Part of His Family

QUESTION 1: EXAMINING GOD'S CHARACTER

How would your life and purpose be affected if God had **not** graciously chosen you to be part of the Body of Christ?

---

[8] Charles R. Swindoll, *The Grace Awakening* (Dallas, TX: Word Publishing, 1990), p. 112.

QUESTION 2: CURRENT CIRCUMSTANCES

How does knowing that you were chosen by God bring confidence and assurance when you face challenges or doubts about your worth?

QUESTION 3: FUTURE PLANS - KNOWING THIS TRUTH

How can you live out your identity as one of God's chosen people, demonstrating His love and purpose in your daily life?

A Prayer of Gratitude for Being Chosen by God

Heavenly Father,

Thank You for graciously choosing me to be part of the Body of Christ. I am humbled and filled with awe that You, in Your sovereignty, have called me into Your family. Help me to trust in Your love and purpose for my life, especially in moments of doubt.

Teach me to reflect my identity as one of Your chosen people by living with purpose, compassion, kindness, humility, and patience. May my life glorify You and draw others to Your saving grace.

In Jesus's Name,
Amen.

8. You Can Call God Abba Father

Scripture

Romans 8:15-16 "The Spirit you received does not make you slaves, so that you live in fear again; rather, the Spirit you received brought about your adoption to sonship. And by him we cry, 'Abba, Father.' The Spirit himself testifies with our spirit that we are God's children." (NIV)

Highlights

- **Transformational Truth:** At the moment of salvation, you are brought into God's family and given the status of sons and daughters, allowed to call God your "Father."
- **Foundational Word:** "Father" (*Greek: Patēr*) signifies an intimate and personal relationship with God, reflecting His care, authority, and love. "Abba" (ἀββα) is an Aramaic term that expresses intimacy, similar to "Daddy" or "Papa" in English, and is used alongside "Patēr" in the New Testament to emphasize the deep, personal relationship believers have with God.
- **Theological Insight**: Erwin Lutzer shares, "The ability to call God 'Abba, Father' is the hallmark of our adoption into His family, a relationship defined by His grace and our intimate fellowship with Him."[9]

Grace Power-Up: Can Call God "Abba Father"

QUESTION 1: EXAMINING GOD'S CHARACTER

How would your relationship with God be different if He had **not** given you the intimate privilege of calling Him "Abba, Father?"

---

[9] Erwin W. Lutzer, *The Cross in the Shadow of the Crescent* (Eugene, OR: Harvest House Publishers, 2013), p. 132.

QUESTION 2: CURRENT CIRCUMSTANCES

How does knowing you can call God "Abba, Father" bring comfort and reassurance during times of fear, loneliness, or uncertainty?

_____

_____

_____

QUESTION 3: FUTURE PLANS - KNOWING THIS TRUTH

How can you live each day in the confidence of being God's beloved child, deepening your relationship with Him through prayer and trust?

_____

_____

_____

A Prayer of Gratitude for Calling God "Abba, Father"

Heavenly Father,

Thank You for bringing me into Your family and giving me the incredible privilege of calling You "Abba, Father." I am overwhelmed by Your love and grace that invites me into such an intimate relationship with You. Help me to rest in the assurance of being Your child, especially in moments of fear or doubt.

Teach me to grow closer to You each day, trusting in Your care and authority over my life. May my relationship with You inspire others to seek the joy and peace of being called Your sons and daughters.

In Jesus's Name,
Amen.

9. You Are a Citizen of Heaven

Scripture

Philippians 3:20 "But our citizenship is in heaven. And we eagerly await a Savior from there, the Lord Jesus Christ." (NIV)

Highlights

- **Transformational Truth:** At the moment of salvation, you become citizens of heaven, eagerly awaiting our savior Jesus Christ.
- **Foundational Word:** "Citizenship" (Greek: *politeuma*) refers to the legal status of belonging to a community or state.
- **Theological Insight:** F.F. Bruce explains, "Believers' citizenship is in heaven, where their names are registered, and their ultimate loyalty resides."[10]

Grace Power-Up: Heavenly Citizenship

QUESTION 1: EXAMINING GOD'S CHARACTER

How would your sense of belonging and purpose be impacted if God had **not** granted you citizenship in heaven?

_____

_____

_____

---

[10] F.F. Bruce, *The Epistle to the Philippians* (Grand Rapids, MI: Eerdmans, 1983), p. 104.

QUESTION 2: CURRENT CIRCUMSTANCES

How does knowing your ultimate citizenship is in heaven help you navigate the challenges and distractions of life on earth?

___

___

___

QUESTION 3: FUTURE PLANS - KNOWING THIS TRUTH

How can you live as a citizen of heaven, reflecting the values and priorities of the Body of Christ in your daily life?

___

___

___

A Prayer of Gratitude for Heavenly Citizenship

Heavenly Father,

Thank You for granting me citizenship in heaven and members in the Body of Christ. I am grateful for the assurance of belonging to You and eagerly await the return of my Savior, Jesus Christ.

Help me to live as an ambassador for You as a member of the Body of Christ, reflecting You in all I do. May my life point others to the joy and hope of being part of the Body of Christ and Christ as the head.

In Jesus's Name,
Amen.

10. You Are Called a Saint

Scripture

1 Corinthians 1:2 "To the church of God which is at Corinth, to those sanctified in Christ Jesus, called to be saints together with all those who in every place call on the name of our Lord Jesus Christ, both their Lord and ours." (RSV)

Highlights

- **Transformational Truth:** At the moment of salvation, you are called saints, set apart by God and made holy through Christ.
- **Foundational Word:** "Saints" (*Greek: hagios*) means holy ones or those set apart, signifying the believer's new identity in Christ as part of His sanctified people.
- **Theological Insight:** John Calvin states, "To be called a saint is not based on human merit but on the sanctifying work of the Spirit and the imputed righteousness of Christ."[11]

Grace Power-Up: Called Saints

QUESTION 1: EXAMINING GOD'S CHARACTER

How would your understanding of God's grace and love change if He had **not** set you apart as a saint, leaving you to rely on your own merit to be considered holy?

___

___

___

---

[11] John Calvin, *Institutes of the Christian Religion*, Book III, Chapter 11, Section 6 (Edinburgh: Calvin Translation Society, 1845).

QUESTION 2: CURRENT CIRCUMSTANCES

How does embracing your identity as a saint, sanctified in Christ, encourage you to live a life that reflects His holiness and purpose?

_____

_____

_____

QUESTION 3: FUTURE PLANS - KNOWING THIS TRUTH

How can you actively walk in your identity as a saint, using your set-apart life to glorify God and serve others?

_____

_____

_____

A Prayer of Gratitude for Being Called a Saint

Heavenly Father,

Thank You for calling me a saint, setting me apart through the righteousness of Christ and the work of Your Spirit. I am humbled and grateful for this new identity that is not based on my merit but on Your grace and love.

Help me to live a life worthy of this calling, reflecting Your holiness and purpose in all I do. Teach me to embrace this identity and to use my life to glorify You and to be a blessing to others.

In Jesus's Name,
Amen.

The Work of Christ

11. You Are Redeemed by Christ's Blood

Scripture

Ephesians 1:7 "In him we have redemption through his blood, the forgiveness of sins, in accordance with the riches of God's grace." (NIV)

Highlights

- **Transformational Truth:** At the moment of salvation, you receive redemption through Christ, rescued from the bondage of sin and brought back into a restored relationship with God.

- **Foundational Word:** "Redeemed" (Greek: apolytrōsis) refers to the act of being set free through a ransom paid.

- **Theological Insight:** John Stott writes, "Redemption emphasizes the costly price of our freedom, fully paid by Christ's sacrifice on the cross."[12]

Grace Power-Up: Redemption Through Christ

QUESTION 1: EXAMINING GOD'S CHARACTER

Where would you remain if God had **not** paid the ransom through Christ to redeem you from the bondage of sin?

_____

_____

_____

---

[12] John Stott, *The Cross of Christ* (Downers Grove, IL: IVP Books, 1986), p. 162.

QUESTION 2: CURRENT CIRCUMSTANCES

How does knowing you have been redeemed through Christ's sacrifice give you strength to overcome struggles or feelings of unworthiness?

_____

_____

_____

QUESTION 3: FUTURE PLANS - KNOWING THIS TRUTH

How can you live in a way that reflects gratitude for the costly price of your redemption?

_____

_____

_____

A Prayer of Gratitude for Redemption Through Christ

Heavenly Father,

Thank You for redeeming me through the precious blood of Jesus Christ. I am overwhelmed by the grace that set me free from the bondage of sin and restored me to a relationship with You. Help me to live in the freedom and joy of this redemption every day.

Teach me to reflect Your love and grace to others, sharing the hope and truth of redemption. May my life honor the sacrifice You made to bring me back to You.

In Jesus's Name,
Amen.

12. Your Sins Are Forgiven

Scripture

Ephesians 1:7 "In him we have redemption through his blood, the forgiveness of sins, in accordance with the riches of God's grace." (NIV)

Highlights

- **Transformational Truth:** At the moment of salvation, you are forgiven of all sins through the atoning work of Christ.
- **Foundational Word:** "Forgiven" (Greek: *aphiēmi*) means to send away or release, signifying the complete removal of guilt.
- **Theological Insight:** Charles Spurgeon: "Forgiveness is a divine act of God's mercy and grace where our sins are remembered no more."[13]

Grace Power-Up: Forgiveness of Sins

QUESTION 1: EXAMINING GOD'S CHARACTER

How would your life look if God chose **not** to offer forgiveness, leaving you to carry the full weight of your guilt and sin?

_____

_____

_____

---

[13] Charles Spurgeon, *All of Grace* (London: Passmore and Alabaster, 1886), p. 67.

QUESTION 2: CURRENT CIRCUMSTANCES

How does knowing that your sins are completely forgiven help you let go of guilt and embrace freedom today?

_____

_____

_____

QUESTION 3: FUTURE PLANS - KNOWING THIS TRUTH

How can you extend forgiveness to someone in your life as a reflection of the forgiveness you've received?

_____

_____

_____

A Prayer of Gratitude for Forgiveness

Heavenly Father,

Thank You for the gift of forgiveness through the atoning work of Jesus Christ. I am humbled and grateful that You have removed my guilt and set me free from sin. Teach me to live in the freedom of this forgiveness and to let go of any burdens of shame or regret.

Help me to reflect Your mercy by forgiving others as You have forgiven me. May my life be a testament to Your grace and draw others to the joy of knowing You.

In Jesus's Name,
Amen.

13. Your Sins Are Fully Atoned

Scripture

Leviticus 17:11 "For the life of a creature is in the blood, and I have given it to you to make atonement for yourselves on the altar; it is the blood that makes atonement for one's life." (NIV) (While the Old Testament primarily foreshadows and points towards salvation through Christ, the Messiah, it provides foundational principles that describe God's redemptive work at the moment of salvation.)

Romans 3:25-26 "God presented Christ as a sacrifice of atonement, through the shedding of his blood—to be received by faith. He did this to demonstrate his righteousness, because in his forbearance he had left the sins committed beforehand unpunished—he did it to demonstrate his righteousness at the present time, so as to be just and the one who justifies those who have faith in Jesus." (NIV)

Highlights

- **Transformational Truth:** At the moment of salvation, God through the perfect Blood of Jesus Christ provides a one-time atonement for sin through a substitutionary sacrifice.
- **Foundational Word:** "Atonement" (Hebrew: *kaphar*) means to cover or reconcile.
- **Theological Insight**: John MacArthur notes, "The sacrifices in the Old Testament foreshadowed the ultimate atonement made by Christ on the cross."[14]

Grace Power-Up: Atonement for Sin

QUESTION 1: EXAMINING GOD'S CHARACTER

Where would you stand before God if He had **not** provided atonement for your sins through the perfect sacrifice of Jesus Christ?

---

[14] John MacArthur, *The MacArthur Study Bible* (Nashville, TN: Thomas Nelson, 1997), commentary on Hebrews 10:1-10.

QUESTION 2: CURRENT CIRCUMSTANCES

How does knowing that Christ's blood has fully atoned for your sins bring you peace and freedom from guilt?

QUESTION 3: FUTURE PLANS - KNOWING THIS TRUTH

How can you live in a way that reflects gratitude for Christ's sacrifice, sharing the message of atonement with others?

A Prayer of Gratitude for Atonement

Heavenly Father,

Thank You for providing atonement for my sins through the blood of Jesus Christ. I am in awe of the sacrifice that reconciles me to You and covers my sin and pays my debt once and for all. Help me to live in the freedom and joy of this truth, fully trusting in Your grace.

Teach me to share this message of redeeming atonement with others and to live in a way that honors the sacrifice of Christ. May my life reflect the transformative power of Your atonement.

In Jesus's Name,
Amen.

14. Christ Paid the Penalty for Your Sin

Scripture

2 Corinthians 5:21 "God made him who had no sin to be sin for us, so that in him we might become the righteousness of God." (NIV)

Colossians 2:14 "Having canceled the charge of our legal indebtedness, which stood against us and condemned us; he has taken it away, nailing it to the cross." (NIV)

Highlights

- **Transformational Truth:** At the moment of salvation, you are made righteous before God because Christ bore the penalty for your sins, taking your place on the cross. You receive a full pardon and the penalty for your sins is canceled, marked "paid in full" by the purity of Christ's blood sacrifice.

- **Foundational Word:** "Pardon" (*Greek: aphesis*) signifies a release from bondage or imprisonment, forgiveness, or remission of the penalty.

- **Theological Insight:** John MacArthur writes, "Christ's substitutionary death was the great exchange—our sin for His righteousness."[15]

Grace Power-Up: Christ Paid the Penalty for Sin

QUESTION 1: EXAMINING GOD'S CHARACTER

How would your understanding of God's justice and mercy be affected if Christ had **not** taken your place (paid the penalty for your sins and provided a full-pardon), leaving you to bear it yourself?

_____

_____

---

[15] John MacArthur, *The MacArthur New Testament Commentary: 2 Corinthians* (Chicago, IL: Moody Publishers, 2003), p. 236.

QUESTION 2: CURRENT CIRCUMSTANCES

How does knowing that Christ bore the penalty for your sins give you peace and assurance, especially when you face guilt or feelings of unworthiness?

QUESTION 3: FUTURE PLANS - KNOWING THIS TRUTH

How can you live in gratitude for Christ's sacrifice, sharing the message of His atonement with others and walking in His righteousness?

A Prayer of Gratitude for Christ Paying the Penalty for Sin

Heavenly Father, thank You for sending Christ to bear the penalty for my sins, taking my place on the cross and granting me His righteousness. I am deeply grateful for the great exchange that made me righteous before You through His sacrifice.

Help me to live in the peace and freedom of knowing my debt has been paid in full. Teach me to reflect this gratitude in my words and actions, sharing the message of salvation with others and glorifying You through a life transformed by grace.

In Jesus's Name,

Amen.

15. You Are Given a Crown of Righteousness

Scripture

1 Corinthians 9:25 "Everyone who competes in the games goes into strict training. They do it to get a crown that will not last, but we do it to get a crown that will last forever." (NIV)

2 Timothy 4:8 "Now there is in store for me the crown of righteousness, which the Lord, the righteous Judge, will award to me on that day—and not only to me, but also to all who have longed for his appearing." (NIV)

Highlights

- **Transformational Truth:** At the moment of salvation, you are set on a path toward receiving the crown of righteousness, a reward promised to believers. This crown is not earned by works but given by the grace of God as a declaration of your right standing with Him.
- **Foundational Word:** "Crown" (Greek: *stephanos*) refers to a victor's wreath, a symbol of triumph, honor, and reward. It signifies the eternal recognition believers receive from the righteous Judge.
- **Theological Insight**: Mark Batterson shares, "There is a similar instinct hardwired into the human soul—the longing to be blessed by God."[16]

Grace Power-Up: Given a Crown of Righteousness

QUESTION 1: EXAMINING GOD'S CHARACTER

What does it reveal about God's nature that He promises a crown of righteousness, not for our works, but as an act of His grace?

_____

_____

---

[16] Batterson, Mark. (2020, August 5). *Nostalgia for God*. [Blog post]. Retrieved from https://www.markbatterson.com/nostalgia-for-god/

QUESTION 2: CURRENT CIRCUMSTANCES

How does knowing a crown of righteousness is awaiting you inspire you to live with greater faithfulness and anticipation for Christ's return?

QUESTION 3: FUTURE PLANS - KNOWING THIS TRUTH

What practical steps can you take to live in a way that reflects your longing for Christ's appearing and looking forward to Christ Himself placing a Crown of Righteousness on your head?

A Prayer of Gratitude for the Crown of Righteousness

Heavenly Father,

Thank You for the promise of the crown of righteousness, a reward of grace for all who trust in You. I am humbled that You, the righteous Judge, would bestow on me such an honor.

Help me to live faithfully and intentionally, keeping my eyes fixed on Jesus and the hope of His appearing. Teach me to value eternal rewards above earthly treasures, and may my life reflect the righteousness You have given to me in Christ.

In Jesus's Name,
Amen.

...back...and fell de...
...giving...16 and...
...aritan. 17 And Jesus an...
...were there not ten cleansed?...
...the nine? 18 There are not...
...eturned to give glory to God,...
...ranger. 19 And he said unto

The Role of the Holy Spirit

16. You Are Baptized into the Body by the Holy Spirit

Scripture

1 Corinthians 12:12–13 "For in one Spirit we were all baptized into one body—whether Jews or Greeks, slave or free—and we were all given the one Spirit to drink." (NIV)

Highlights

- **Transformational Truth:** At the moment of salvation, you are baptized (a dry baptism) into the Body of Christ by the Holy Spirit.
- **Foundational Word:** "Baptized" (*Greek: baptizo*) signifies the Holy Spirit's work, (a non-water baptism), symbolizing the believer's identification with Christ's death, burial, and resurrection.
- **Theological Insight**: D.L. Moody shares, "The baptism of the Holy Spirit is not about water but about power—His power to unite us to Christ and to each other in His Body."[17]

Grace Power-Up: Baptism by the Holy Spirit

QUESTION 1: EXAMINING GOD'S CHARACTER

How would your life and sense of belonging be different if God had **not** united you to Christ and His Body through the baptism of the Holy Spirit?

_____

_____

_____

---

[17] D.L. Moody, *Secret Power: The Secret of Success in Christian Life and Work* (Chicago, IL: Fleming H. Revell Company, 1881), p. 49.

QUESTION 2: CURRENT CIRCUMSTANCES

How does knowing you are spiritually united with other believers by the Holy Spirit encourage you in moments of loneliness or division?

_____

_____

_____

QUESTION 3: FUTURE PLANS - KNOWING THIS TRUTH

How can you actively contribute to unity within the Body of Christ, reflecting the work of the Holy Spirit?

_____

_____

_____

A Prayer of Gratitude for Baptism by the Holy Spirit

Heavenly Father, thank You for baptizing me into the Body of Christ through the Holy Spirit. I am grateful for the unity, belonging, and power that come from Your Spirit to be a member of the Body of Christ. Help me to live in harmony with other members of the unique group of believers, celebrating our shared connection in You.

Teach me to walk in the Spirit daily, contributing to unity and glorifying You in my relationships and actions. May my life reflect the transformative power of being a part this new Body of Christ.

In Jesus's Name,
Amen.

17. You Are Indwelt by the Holy Spirit

Scripture

1 Corinthians 6:19 "Do you not know that your bodies are temples of the Holy Spirit, who is in you, whom you have received from God? You are not your own." (NIV)

Highlights

- **Transformational Truth:** At the moment of salvation, you receive the indwelling presence of the Holy Spirit.

- **Foundational Word:** "Indwelt" (Greek: enoikeō) means to dwell within or take up residence, signifying the Holy Spirit's abiding presence in the believer.

- **Theological Insight:** Billy Graham: "The Holy Spirit's indwelling transforms the heart and empowers the believer for godly living."[18]

Grace Power-Up: Indwelling of the Holy Spirit

QUESTION 1: EXAMINING GOD'S CHARACTER

How would your life differ if God had **not** given you the Holy Spirit to dwell within you, guiding and empowering you for godly living?

_____

_____

_____

---

[18] Billy Graham, *The Holy Spirit: Activating God's Power in Your Life* (Nashville, TN: Thomas Nelson, 1978), p. 104.

QUESTION 2: CURRENT CIRCUMSTANCES

How does knowing the Holy Spirit resides in you help you face challenges or gives comfort and strength when weak in your daily life?

_____

_____

_____

QUESTION 3: FUTURE PLANS - KNOWING THIS TRUTH

In what ways can you intentionally live as a temple of the Holy Spirit, honoring God in your thoughts, words, and actions?

_____

_____

_____

A Prayer of Gratitude for the Holy Spirit's Work

Heavenly Father,

Thank You for the incredible gift of the Holy Spirit, who dwells within me. I am humbled to know that my body is a temple of Your presence. Help me to live in a way that honors and reflects Your holiness and guidance.

Teach me to rely on the Spirit's power in every area of my life, facing challenges with courage and living with purpose. May Your Spirit transform my heart and lead me in the path of righteousness for Your glory.

In Jesus's Name,
Amen.

18. You Are Sanctified by the Spirit

Scripture

1 Corinthians 6:11 "But you were washed, you were sanctified, you were justified in the name of the Lord Jesus Christ and by the Spirit of our God." (NIV)

Highlights

- **Transformational Truth:** At the moment of salvation, you are set apart for God's purposes through the work of the Holy Spirit.
- **Foundational Word:** "Sanctified" (Greek: *hagiazō*) means to make holy or set apart.
- **Theological Insight:** John Calvin: "Sanctification is the Spirit's ongoing work to conform us to Christ."[19]

Grace Power-Up: Sanctification by the Spirit

QUESTION 1: EXAMINING GOD'S CHARACTER

What would your life look like if God had **not** set you apart through the Holy Spirit to grow in holiness and fulfill His purposes?

_____

_____

_____

---

[19] John Calvin, *Institutes of the Christian Religion*, Book III, Chapter 3, Section 9 (Edinburgh: Calvin Translation Society, 1845).

QUESTION 2: CURRENT CIRCUMSTANCES

How does knowing that the Holy Spirit is actively sanctifying you help you face struggles or temptations in your daily walk?

_____

_____

_____

QUESTION 3: FUTURE PLANS - KNOWING THIS TRUTH

How can you cooperate with the Spirit's work to grow in Christlikeness and reflect God's holiness in your life?

_____

_____

_____

A Prayer of Gratitude for Sanctification by the Spirit

Heavenly Father,

Thank You for sanctifying me through the work of Your Holy Spirit. I am grateful to be set apart for Your purposes, and I trust in Your ongoing work to conform me to the image of Christ. Help me to rely on Your Spirit as I face struggles and seek to live a holy life.

Teach me to surrender to Your guidance daily and to reflect Your holiness in all I do. May my life glorify You and encourage others to seek Your transforming power.

In Jesus's Name,
Amen.

19. You Have the Power to Love Fully

Scripture

1 Corinthians 13:4–7 "Love is patient, love is kind, it is not jealous; love does not brag, it is not arrogant. It does not act disgracefully, it does not seek its own benefit; it is not provoked, does not keep an account of a wrong suffered, it does not rejoice in unrighteousness, but rejoices with the truth; it keeps every confidence, it believes all things, hopes all things, endures all things." (NASB)

Highlights

- **Transformational Truth:** At the moment of salvation, you are given the power to love fully as the Lord loves. This love is sacrificial, selfless, and seeks the well-being of others, reflecting the transformative nature of God's love in us.
- **Foundational Word:** "Love" (Greek: *agapē*) signifies a divine, unconditional love characterized by selflessness and sacrifice.
- **Theological Insight:** John Stott writes, "True love is not self-seeking but seeks to mirror God's love, which is patient, kind, and enduring."[20]

Grace Power-Up: The Power to "Agape" - Love Fully

QUESTION 1: EXAMINING GOD'S CHARACTER

How would your understanding of love and relationships differ if God had **not** demonstrated sacrificial and selfless love toward you?

_____

_____

_____

---

[20] John Stott, *The Message of 1 Corinthians: Life in the Local Church* (Downers Grove, IL: InterVarsity Press, 1985), p. 222.

QUESTION 2: CURRENT CIRCUMSTANCES

How does reflecting on God's love help you respond to situations where loving someone feels difficult or undeserved?

_____

_____

_____

QUESTION 3: FUTURE PLANS - KNOWING THIS TRUTH

How can you intentionally show sacrificial love in a specific relationship or situation this week?

_____

_____

_____

A Prayer to Love as God Loves

Heavenly Father,

Thank You for showing me the depth of Your love through Jesus Christ. I am humbled by the selfless and sacrificial love You give and the power You have placed in me to love as You do. Help me to reflect Your love, especially when it is difficult, and teach me to seek the well-being of others above my own.

Empower me to love fully, showing patience, kindness, and grace in every interaction. May my love point others toward You and glorify Your name.

In Jesus's Name,
Amen.

20. You Are Sealed by the Holy Spirit

Scripture

2 Corinthians 1:22 "Set his seal of ownership on us, and put his Spirit in our hearts as a deposit, guaranteeing what is to come." (NIV)

Ephesians 1:13 "And you also were included in Christ when you heard the message of truth, the gospel of your salvation. When you believed, you were marked in him with a seal, the promised Holy Spirit." (NIV)

Ephesians 4:30 "And do not grieve the Holy Spirit of God, with whom you were sealed for the day of redemption." (NIV)

Highlights

- **Transformational Truth:** At the moment of salvation, you are sealed by the Holy Spirit, marked as God's own and guaranteeing your eternal inheritance.
- **Foundational Word:** "Sealed" (*Greek: sphragizō*) means to mark with a seal, symbolizing ownership, security, and authenticity, confirming God's covenant with His people.
- **Theological Insight**: John Calvin states, "The sealing of the Spirit is the pledge of our eternal inheritance, a divine guarantee that we belong to God and will share in His glory."[21]

Grace Power-Up: Sealed by the Spirit

QUESTION 1: EXAMINING GOD'S CHARACTER

How would your sense of security and belonging be affected if God had **not** sealed you with His Spirit, leaving you uncertain of your salvation and inheritance?

---

[21] John Calvin, *Institutes of the Christian Religion*, Book III, Chapter 2, Section 11 (Edinburgh: Calvin Translation Society, 1845).

QUESTION 2: CURRENT CIRCUMSTANCES

How does knowing you are marked with the Holy Spirit as God's own give you confidence and peace in your daily walk with Him?

QUESTION 3: FUTURE PLANS - KNOWING THIS TRUTH

How can you live each day with the assurance of being sealed by the Spirit, reflecting your identity as a child of God and heir to His promises?

A Prayer of Gratitude for Being Sealed by the Spirit

Heavenly Father,

Thank You for sealing me with the Holy Spirit, marking me as Your own and guaranteeing my eternal inheritance. I am humbled and grateful for the assurance of Your promise and the security it brings to my life.

Teach me to live confidently in this truth, reflecting my identity as Your child and walking in the peace of knowing I am forever Yours. May my life glorify You and draw others to the joy and hope found in Your promises.

In Jesus's Name,
Amen.

21. You Have Peace with God

Scripture

Romans 5:1 "Therefore, since we have been justified through faith, we have peace with God through our Lord Jesus Christ." (NIV)

Highlights

- **Transformational Truth:** At the moment of salvation, God reconciles you to Himself, ending enmity and establishing a harmonious relationship of peace.

- **Foundational Word:** "Peace" (Greek: *eirēnē*) denotes a state of harmony and wholeness, reflecting the believer's restored relationship with God.

- **Theological Insight:** John Piper writes, "Peace with God is the assurance of salvation and the removal of God's wrath."[22]

Grace Power-Up: Peace with God

QUESTION 1: EXAMINING GOD'S CHARACTER

Where do you think your life would be if God had chosen **not** to reconcile with you, withholding His mercy and offering no way for a relationship with Him?

_____

_____

_____

---

[22] John Piper, *The Future of Justification: A Response to N.T. Wright* (Wheaton, IL: Crossway Books, 2007), p. 64.

QUESTION 2: CURRENT CIRCUMSTANCES

How does knowing you have peace with God give you confidence to face situations where you might otherwise feel anxious?

_____

_____

_____

QUESTION 3: FUTURE PLANS - KNOWING THIS TRUTH

In what ways can the assurance of being at peace with God inspire you to pursue harmony in your relationships with others?

_____

_____

_____

A Prayer of Gratitude for Peace with God

Heavenly Father,

Thank You for reconciling me to Yourself through Jesus Christ. I cannot imagine where I would be without Your mercy and the peace You have given me. Help me to live with confidence and joy, trusting in the assurance of my salvation and Your constant presence in my life.

Teach me to be a peacemaker, reflecting Your grace and harmony in my relationships. May my life point others toward the peace that only You can provide.

In Jesus's Name,
Amen.

22. You Are Given Armor from God to Defend Yourself

Scripture

Ephesians 6:11 "Put on the full armor of God, so that you can take your stand against the devil's schemes." (NIV)

Highlights

- **Transformational Truth:** At the moment of salvation, God equips you with His armor to protect yourself from spiritual attacks. This armor enables you to stand firm in faith, defending yourself against the enemy's schemes, and live victoriously in Christ.

- **Foundational Word:** "Armor" (Greek: *panoplia*) refers to a complete set of protective gear. It emphasizes being fully equipped with the spiritual tools necessary to engage in and withstand the spiritual battles of life.

- **Theological Insight:** Tony Evans explains, "The armor of God is the practical application of God's power in your life. Each piece represents a key aspect of standing firm in the truth, faith, righteousness, and salvation provided by Christ."[23]

Grace Power-Up: The Armor of God

Question 1: Examining God's Character
How does God's provision of spiritual armor reveal His care and commitment to your protection and victory in spiritual battles? (Contemplate your standing without this armor.)

_____

_____

---

[23] Evans, Tony, *Victory in Spiritual Warfare: Outfitting Yourself for the Battle*. Harvest House Publishers, (2011). p. 42.

Question 2: Current Circumstances
How can relying on the armor of God help you stand firm in faith amidst trials and temptations you are facing right now? (Read and consider Isaiah 59:17)

Question 3: Future Plans - Knowing This Truth
What practical steps can you take to intentionally "put on" the armor of God daily and walk in victory over the enemy's schemes?

A Prayer for Strength and Protection with God's Armor

Heavenly Father,

Thank You for equipping me with Your full armor to defend myself against the enemy's schemes. I am grateful for the strength and protection You provide through truth, righteousness, peace, faith, salvation, and the power of Your Word.

Help me to put on this armor daily, standing firm in Your power and living with confidence in the victory You have secured. Teach me to rely on Your Spirit and Your Word as I face spiritual challenges, always remembering that my strength comes from You.

Thank You for being my shield, my sword and my fortress. May my life reflect Your power and glory.

In Jesus's Name, Amen.

23. You Walk as a Child of Light

Scripture

Ephesians 5:8 "For you were once darkness, but now you are light in the Lord. Live as children of light." (NIV)

Highlights

- **Transformational Truth:** At the moment of salvation, you are called to walk as children of light, living in righteousness and spreading the gospel (good news) to the world.
- **Foundational Word:** "Walking" (Greek: *peripateō*) refers to conducting one's life in a manner consistent with their identity in Christ.
- **Theological Insight:** John Stott writes, "To walk as children of light means to live out the character of Christ, shining His truth and love in a dark world."[24]

Grace Power-Up: Walking as a Child of Light

QUESTION 1: EXAMINING GOD'S CHARACTER

How would your life and influence be different if God had left you in darkness, without calling you to walk as a child of light?

_____

_____

_____

---

[24] John Stott, *The Message of Ephesians: God's New Society* (Downers Grove, IL: InterVarsity Press, 1979), p. 198.

QUESTION 2: CURRENT CIRCUMSTANCES

How does knowing you are now light in the Lord encourage you to reflect Christ's truth and love in difficult situations or relationships?

_____

_____

_____

QUESTION 3: FUTURE PLANS - KNOWING THIS TRUTH

How can you intentionally live as a child of light this week, making choices that honor God and shine His light in the world?

_____

_____

_____

A Prayer of Gratitude for Walking as a Child of Light

Heavenly Father,

Thank You for calling me out of darkness and making me light in the Lord. I am grateful for the privilege and responsibility to walk as a child of light, reflecting Your truth, righteousness, and love to the world.

Teach me to live each day in a way that honors You, spreading the light of Christ through my words and actions. May my life be a beacon that points others to Your grace, hope and salvation.

In Jesus's Name,
Amen.

24. You Can Find Contentment through God's Grace

Scripture

Philippians 4:11-13 "I am not saying this because I am in need, for I have learned to be content whatever the circumstances. I know what it is to be in need, and I know what it is to have plenty. I have learned the secret of being content in any and every situation, whether well fed or hungry, whether living in plenty or in want. I can do all this through him who gives me strength." (NIV)

Highlights

- **Transformational Truth:** At the moment of salvation, you are given the profound secret of contentment, made possible by God's abundant grace. This contentment allows you to rest in His provision and sufficiency, regardless of your circumstances.
- **Foundational Word:** "Contentment" (*Greek: autarkeia*) refers to a state of sufficiency, satisfaction, and peace, derived from reliance on God's provision rather than external circumstances.
- **Theological Insight:** D.L. Moody says, "Contentment is not about having what we want, but wanting what God provides, resting in the assurance of His grace and faithfulness."[25]

Grace Power-Up: Finding Contentment through God's Grace

QUESTION 1: EXAMINING GOD'S CHARACTER

How would your peace and satisfaction in life be affected if God's grace were **not** sufficient to sustain you in every circumstance, leaving you dependent on external conditions for contentment?

---

[25] D.L. Moody, *The Overcoming Life* (Chicago, IL: Fleming H. Revell Company, 1896), p. 87.

QUESTION 2: CURRENT CIRCUMSTANCES

How does relying on God's grace and provision help you find contentment, even in situations of persecution, uncertainty, or difficulty?

___

___

QUESTION 3: FUTURE PLANS - KNOWING THIS TRUTH

How can you intentionally cultivate a heart of contentment, trusting God's grace to meet your needs and resting in His sufficiency?

___

___

A Prayer of Gratitude for Contentment through God's Grace

Heavenly Father,

Thank You for teaching me the profound secret of contentment through Your grace. I am grateful that my satisfaction and peace come from Your provision, not from my circumstances. Help me to rest in the assurance of Your faithfulness, trusting in Your sufficiency to meet my every need.

Teach me to cultivate a heart of gratitude and embracing contentment, reflecting confidence in Your grace and provision. May my life demonstrate the peace and joy that come from depending on You, inspiring others to seek the same.

In Jesus's Name,
Amen.

25. You Are Free from the Burden of Self-Righteousness

Scripture

Ephesians 2:8-9 "For it is by grace you have been saved, through faith—and this is not from yourselves, it is the gift of God—not by works, so that no one can boast." (NIV)

1 Timothy 1:15 "Here is a trustworthy saying that deserves full acceptance: Christ Jesus came into the world to save sinners—of whom I am the worst." (NIV)

Highlights

- **Transformational Truth:** At the moment of salvation, you are liberated from the exhausting and unobtainable burden of self-righteousness, as your acceptance before God is based on Christ's work on the cross rather than your personal performance or works.

- **Foundational Word:** "Save" (Greek: *sōzō*) means to rescue or deliver, highlighting Christ's complete work on behalf of sinners.

- **Theological Insight**: C.R. Stam shares, "Grace sets us free from striving for self-righteousness, revealing the complete sufficiency of Christ's work for our salvation. We are called not to work for salvation but to rest in what He has already accomplished."[26]

Grace Power-Up: Freedom from the Burden of Self-Righteousness

QUESTION 1: EXAMINING GOD'S CHARACTER

How would your relationship with God change if your acceptance before Him depended on your own works rather than the sufficiency of Christ's sacrifice?

---

[26] C.R. Stam, *Things That Differ: The Fundamentals of Dispensationalism* (Germantown, WI: Berean Bible Society, 1951), p. 157.

QUESTION 2: CURRENT CIRCUMSTANCES

How does knowing your salvation is secured by Christ's work, not your own efforts, free you from the pressure of striving for self-righteousness?

QUESTION 3: FUTURE PLANS - KNOWING THIS TRUTH

How can you live out the freedom of grace, demonstrating humility and gratitude while pointing others to Christ's sufficiency rather than self-effort?

A Prayer of Gratitude for Freedom from Self-Righteousness

Heavenly Father,

Thank You for liberating me from the burden of self-righteousness. I am grateful that my acceptance before You is based entirely on Christ's finished work on the cross and not my flawed efforts. Help me to rest in Your grace and to live in the freedom that comes from trusting in Your sufficiency.

Teach me to reflect this freedom through humility, gratitude, and love, pointing others to the truth that salvation is a gift and not earned by human effort. May my life glorify You and magnify the beauty of Your grace.

In Jesus's Name, Amen.

God's Grace and Sovereignty

26. You Are Eternally Secure in Christ

Scripture

John 10:28-29 "I give them eternal life, and they shall never perish; no one will snatch them out of my hand. My Father, who has given them to me, is greater than all; no one can snatch them out of my Father's hand" (NIV)

Ephesians 1:13 "And you also were included in Christ when you heard the message of truth, the gospel of your salvation. When you believed, you were marked in him with a seal, the promised Holy Spirit." (NIV)

Philippians 1:6 "Being confident of this, that he who began a good work in you will carry it on to completion until the day of Christ Jesus." (NIV)

Highlights

- **Transformational Truth:** At the moment of salvation, you are secured in Christ, ensuring your salvation for all eternity. This security is grounded in God's unchanging nature and Christ's finished work on the cross.
- **Foundational Word:** "Secure" (Greek: *sozo*) means to save completely and preserve, highlighting God's power to protect and sustain believers.
- **Theological Insight:** R.C. Sproul states, "Eternal security is rooted in God's unchanging nature and Christ's finished work."[27]

Grace Power-Up: Eternal Security in Christ

QUESTION 1: EXAMINING GOD'S CHARACTER

How would your faith and hope be affected if God's promise of eternal security depended on your efforts rather than His unchanging nature?

_____

_____

_____

---

[27] R.C. Sproul, *Chosen by God* (Wheaton, IL: Tyndale House Publishers, 1986), p. 150.

QUESTION 2: CURRENT CIRCUMSTANCES

How does knowing that you are securely held in Christ bring peace and confidence in moments of doubt or fear?

_____

_____

_____

QUESTION 3: FUTURE PLANS - KNOWING THIS TRUTH

How can the assurance of eternal security inspire you to live boldly for Christ, trusting in His ongoing work in your life?

_____

_____

_____

A Prayer of Gratitude for Eternal Security in Christ

Heavenly Father,

Thank You for the eternal security I have in Christ. I am comforted by the assurance that my salvation is held firmly in Your hands and rooted in Your unchanging nature. Help me to trust fully in Your promise, especially in times of doubt or fear.

Teach me to live with boldness and gratitude, reflecting the confidence that comes from being securely Yours. May my life glorify You and draw others to the truth of Your faithfulness.

In Jesus's Name,
Amen.

27. You Are Looking for the Blessed Hope and Glorious Appearing

Scripture

Titus 2:13 "While we wait for the blessed hope—the appearing of the glory of our great God and Savior, Jesus Christ." (NIV)

Highlights

- **Transformational Truth:** At the moment of salvation, believers are called to eagerly anticipate the blessed hope of Christ's glorious return. This future event not only secures eternal joy but also transforms how we live in the present world.

- **Foundational Word:** "Blessed Hope" (Greek: *makarios elpis*) combines *makarios* (blessed, joyful, fulfilled) and *elpis* (hope, confident expectation). Together, the phrase signifies a deep and joyful anticipation of God's ultimate promise: Christ's return and the believer's eternal fellowship with Him.

- **Theological Insight**: Billy Graham's quote, "The end will come with the return of Jesus Christ...That is why a Christian can be an optimist. That is why a Christian can smile in the midst of all that is happening...We know what the end will be: the triumph of the Lord Jesus Christ,"[28]

Grace Power-Up: Looking for the Blessed Hope and Glorious Appearing

QUESTION 1: EXAMINING GOD'S CHARACTER

---

[28] Graham, Billy.*New Heaven, New Earth*. Billy Graham Evangelistic Association. (2011, May 9). Retrieved from https://billygraham.org/devotion/new-heaven-new-earth/

What would it look like if there was no promise of Christ's return and God's character and promised of His return could **not** be trusted?

___

___

___

QUESTION 2: CURRENT CIRCUMSTANCES

How does the anticipation of the blessed hope help you navigate life's trials with confidence and purpose?

___

___

___

QUESTION 3: FUTURE PLANS - KNOWING THIS TRUTH

What steps can you take to live with a focus on Christ's return, allowing this hope to shape your priorities and your witness to others?

___

___

A Prayer of Gratitude for the Hope of Christ's Appearing

Heavenly Father,

Thank You for the promise of the blessed hope and the glorious appearing of Jesus Christ. I am grateful for the joy and confidence this hope brings, reminding me that Your plans are perfect and eternal.

Teach me to live with eager anticipation, allowing this hope to guide my choices and shape my actions. Help me to reflect Your grace and holiness as I await the fulfillment of Your promises. Strengthen my faith to remain steadfast and joyful, even in the face of trials, knowing that Christ will return to take me to Himself.

In Jesus's Name, Amen.

28. You Are Predestined in Christ

Scripture

Romans 8:29-30 "For those God foreknew he also predestined to be conformed to the image of his Son, that he might be the firstborn among many brothers and sisters. And those he predestined, he also called; those he called, he also justified; those he justified, he also glorified." (NIV)

Ephesians 1:5 & 11 "He predestined us for adoption to sonship through Jesus Christ, in accordance with his pleasure and will."; "In him we were also chosen, having been predestined according to the plan of him who works out everything in conformity with the purpose of his will." (NIV)

Highlights

- **Transformational Truth:** At the moment of salvation, you were predestined by God to be conformed to the image of His Son, according to His eternal purpose and will.
- **Foundational Word:** "Predestined" (*Greek: proorizō*) means to determine beforehand or to ordain in advance, reflecting God's sovereign plan for salvation.
- **Theological Insight:** Charles Baker shares, "Predestination is the expression of God's sovereign will, whereby He lovingly ordains believers to be part of His family and to share in the glory of His Son."[29]

Grace Power-Up: Predestined in Christ

QUESTION 1: EXAMINING GOD'S CHARACTER

How would your understanding of God's love and purpose be affected if He had **not** lovingly predestined you to be conformed to the image of His Son?

---

[29] Charles F. Baker, *A Dispensational Theology* (Grand Rapids, MI: Grace Bible College Publications, 1971), p. 348.

QUESTION 2: CURRENT CIRCUMSTANCES

How does knowing you were predestined by God give you assurance and peace when you face doubts about your place in His plan?

QUESTION 3: FUTURE PLANS - KNOWING THIS TRUTH

How can the knowledge of being predestined to God's family motivate you to live with purpose and reflect His love to others?

A Prayer of Gratitude for Being Predestined in Christ

Heavenly Father,

Thank You for lovingly predestining me to be conformed to the image of Your Son according to Your eternal purpose and will. I am humbled by Your sovereignty and grace that chose me before I even knew You. Help me to trust in Your plan, especially when I face uncertainties and doubts.

Teach me to live in the confidence of being Your child, sharing Your love and reflecting Your purpose to those around me. May my life glorify You as I rest in the assurance of Your eternal will.

In Jesus's Name,
Amen.

29. You Are Fully Accepted by God

Scripture

Romans 8:1 "Therefore, there is now no condemnation for those who are in Christ Jesus." (NIV)

Ephesians 1:6 "To the praise of the glory of His grace, with which He freely bestowed on us in the Beloved." (NASB)

Highlights

- **Transformational Truth:** At the moment of salvation, you are made acceptable to God through Jesus Christ, no longer under condemnation.
- **Foundational Word:** "Accepted" (Greek: *eucharistos*, or in some contexts, *charitoō*) means to be made favorable or pleasing.
- **Theological Insight**: John Stott states, "Our acceptance by God is rooted in Christ's righteousness, imputed to us, making us pleasing in His sight."[30]

Grace Power-Up: Acceptance by God

QUESTION 1: EXAMINING GOD'S CHARACTER

How would your relationship with God be different if He had **not** made you acceptable through Christ, leaving you under condemnation?

_____

_____

_____

---

[30] John Stott, *The Cross of Christ* (Downers Grove, IL: InterVarsity Press, 1986), p. 199.

QUESTION 2: CURRENT CIRCUMSTANCES

How does knowing you are fully accepted by God, with no condemnation, give you peace and confidence when facing feelings of unworthiness or guilt?

_____

_____

_____

QUESTION 3: FUTURE PLANS - KNOWING THIS TRUTH

How can you live with gratitude and assurance, reflecting God's acceptance of you in how you treat others and yourself?

_____

_____

_____

A Prayer of Gratitude for Acceptance by God

Heavenly Father,

Thank You for accepting me through Jesus Christ, removing all condemnation and making me pleasing in Your sight. I am humbled by the grace that has made me favorable to You, not by my works, but by Christ's righteousness imputed to me.

Help me to live with peace and confidence, free from guilt and fear, knowing I am fully accepted by You. Teach me to reflect Your grace and acceptance in my relationships, pointing others to the love found in Christ.

In Jesus's Name,
Amen.

30. You Are Reconciled to God

Scripture

2 Corinthians 5:18-19 "All this is from God, who reconciled us to himself through Christ and gave us the ministry of reconciliation: that God was reconciling the world to himself in Christ, not counting people's sins against them. And he has committed to us the message of reconciliation." (NIV)

Highlights

- **Transformational Truth:** At the moment of salvation, you are reconciled to God, restoring the broken relationship caused by sin.
- **Foundational Word:** "Reconciled" (Greek: *katallassō*) means to bring into harmony, to restore favor or friendship.
- **Theological Insight:** Charles Hodge explains, "Reconciliation is the removal of the barrier of sin between God and humanity, achieved through Christ's atoning work."[31]

Grace Power-Up: Reconciliation to God

QUESTION 1: EXAMINING GOD'S CHARACTER

How would your relationship with God and your life be impacted if He had **not** removed the barrier of sin and reconciled you to Himself through Christ?

---

[31] Charles Hodge, *Systematic Theology*, Vol. 2 (New York: Scribner, Armstrong & Co., 1873), p. 471.

QUESTION 2: CURRENT CIRCUMSTANCES

How does knowing you are reconciled to God give you peace and confidence when facing feelings of guilt, shame, or distance from Him?

_____

_____

_____

QUESTION 3: FUTURE PLANS - KNOWING THIS TRUTH

How can you embrace the ministry of reconciliation, sharing the message of God's grace and restoring relationships in your own life?

_____

_____

_____

A Prayer of Gratitude for Reconciliation to God

Heavenly Father,

Thank You for reconciling me to Yourself through Christ. I am grateful for the removal of the barrier of sin and the restoration of my relationship with You. Help me to live in the peace and joy of this reconciliation, trusting in Your love and forgiveness.

Teach me to share the message of reconciliation with others and to reflect Your grace in my relationships. May my life glorify You as I live out the harmony and favor You have given me through Christ.

In Jesus's Name,
Amen.

The Believer's Privileges

31. You Are Added to the Body of Believers

Scripture

Romans 12:4-5 "For just as each of us has one body with many members, and these members do not all have the same function, so in Christ we, though many, form one body, and each member belongs to all the others." (NIV)

Highlights

- **Transformational Truth:** At the moment of salvation, you are added into the community of faith, called the Body of Christ, with Christ as the head.
- **Foundational Word:** "Added" (*Greek: prostithemi*) means to place or join, signifying the intentional and integral inclusion of each believer into the Body of Christ.
- **Theological Insight**: A.W. Tozer: "The church is a spiritual house where every believer has a role in God's redemptive plan."[32]

Grace Power-Up: Added to the Body of Believers

QUESTION 1: EXAMINING GOD'S CHARACTER

What would your spiritual journey look like if God had **not** intentionally placed you within the community of believers to grow, serve, and find support?

_____

_____

_____

---

[32] A.W. Tozer, *The Purpose of Man: Designed to Worship* (Ventura, CA: Regal Books, 2009), p. 174.

QUESTION 2: CURRENT CIRCUMSTANCES

How does knowing you belong to a body of believers (the Church—the Body of Christ, the worldwide body of believers) encourage you to find purpose and connection, especially during challenging times?

_____

_____

_____

QUESTION 3: FUTURE PLANS - KNOWING THIS TRUTH

How can you actively participate in and contribute to the Body of Christ, using your unique gifts to serve others and glorify God?

_____

_____

_____

A Prayer of Gratitude for Being Added to the Body of Believers

Heavenly Father, thank You for adding me to the body of believers. I am grateful for the community of faith (local church) where I can grow, serve, and experience Your love through others. Help me to embrace my role within Your Church (the worldwide body of believers), contributing to unity and purpose in the Body of Christ.

Teach me to love and serve my brothers and sisters in Christ, reflecting Your grace and fulfilling the role You have given me. Prompt me to us these gifts to serve Your body of believers.

May my life bring glory to You as I build up the body of believers and share Your redemptive plan with others.

In Jesus's Name, Amen.

32. You Are Heavenly Associated with God's Creation

Scripture

Ephesians 2:6 "And God raised us up with Christ and seated us with him in the heavenly realms in Christ Jesus." (NIV)

Highlights

- **Transformational Truth:** At the moment of salvation, you are elevated to a position of spiritual association with Christ in the heavenly realms, signifying unity with God and His purposes in creation.

- **Foundational Word:** "Seated" (Greek: *synekathizō*) denotes being spiritually placed with Christ in a position of authority and privilege.

- **Theological Insight:** John MacArthur states, "Being seated with Christ in the heavenly realms means sharing in His victory, His rule, and His eternal purposes."[33]

Grace Power-Up: Heavenly Association with God's Creation

QUESTION 1: EXAMINING GOD'S CHARACTER

How would your understanding of your purpose and value be affected if God had **not** elevated you to share in Christ's position in the heavenly realms?

_____

_____

_____

---

[33] John MacArthur, *The MacArthur New Testament Commentary: Ephesians* (Chicago, IL: Moody Publishers, 1986), p. 98.

QUESTION 2: CURRENT CIRCUMSTANCES

How does knowing you are spiritually seated with Christ in the heavenly realms bring you confidence and peace in facing life's challenges?

_____

_____

_____

QUESTION 3: FUTURE PLANS - KNOWING THIS TRUTH

How can you live in alignment with your heavenly position, embracing God's purposes and reflecting His authority in your actions?

_____

_____

_____

A Prayer of Gratitude for Heavenly Association

Heavenly Father,

Thank You for raising me up with Christ and seating me with Him in the heavenly realms. I am amazed by the privilege of sharing in His victory, His rule, and His eternal purposes. Help me to live confidently in this truth, trusting in Your power and plan.

Teach me to align my life with Your heavenly purposes, reflecting Your glory and walking in the authority You've entrusted to me in Christ. May my life point others to the victory and hope found in You.

In Jesus's Name,
Amen.

33. You Are Anointed and Empowered by God

Scripture

2 Corinthians 1:21-22 "Now it is God who makes both us and you stand firm in Christ. He anointed us, set his seal of ownership on us, and put his Spirit in our hearts as a deposit, guaranteeing what is to come." (NIV)

Highlights

- **Transformational Truth:** At the moment of salvation, God anoints you with His Spirit, marking you as His own and empowering you for His purposes. This divine calling sets you apart to live out His will, equipped with the power and presence of the Holy Spirit.

- **Foundational Word:** "Anointed" (Greek: *chrio*) refers to the act of consecration or being set apart for a divine purpose. It signifies a special empowerment given by God for His service, reflecting the believer's identity and mission in Christ.

- **Theological Insight:** R.T. Kendall writes, "The anointing is the power and presence of the Holy Spirit to fulfill the task God has called you to. It is not just for a chosen few but for all who are in Christ Jesus."[34]

Grace Power-Up: Anointed and Empowered by God

QUESTION 1: EXAMINING GOD'S CHARACTER

How does God's anointing reflect His love and commitment to empowering you for His purposes or what would your life look like if you were **not** anointed?

_____

_____

_____

[34] Kendall, R.T. (1998). *The Anointing: Yesterday, Today, and Tomorrow*. Charisma House, p. 63.

QUESTION 2: CURRENT CIRCUMSTANCES

How can recognizing your anointing by God encourage you to approach challenges with confidence and faith?

QUESTION 3: FUTURE PLANS - KNOWING THIS TRUTH

What steps can you take to live out your divine calling, empowered by the Holy Spirit to impact others for God's glory?

A Prayer of Gratitude for Being Anointed by God

Heavenly Father, thank You for anointing me with Your Holy Spirit, marking me as Your own and empowering me to fulfill Your purposes. I am grateful for the privilege of being set apart for Your glory and the assurance of Your presence in my life.

Help me to live each day aware of this anointing, walking in the power and guidance of the Spirit. Teach me to embrace my divine calling, using the gifts You have given me to serve others and glorify You.

Thank You for the seal of Your Spirit, guaranteeing all that is to come. May my life reflect the joy and purpose of being Yours.

In Jesus's Name, Amen.

34. You Are Given the Title of Ambassador

Scripture

2 Corinthians 5:20 "We are therefore Christ's ambassadors, as though God were making his appeal through us. We implore you on Christ's behalf: Be reconciled to God." (NIV)

Highlights

- **Transformational Truth:** At the moment of salvation, you are entrusted with the role and title of Ambassadors for Christ, representing Him and proclaiming His message of reconciliation to the world.
- **Foundational Word:** "Ambassador" (Greek: *presbeuō*) refers to one who acts as a representative or envoy on behalf of another.
- **Theological Insight:** Dr. Ken Kemper shares, "Believers are entrusted as ambassadors to reflect the heart of Christ, urging others to be reconciled to God through His transformative grace."[35]

Grace Power-Up: Given the Title of Ambassador

QUESTION 1: EXAMINING GOD'S CHARACTER

How would the world miss out on the message of reconciliation if God had **not** entrusted you with the role of ambassador for Christ?

_____

_____

_____

---

[35] Ken Kemper, *Ambassadors of Grace: Living Out Reconciliation in a Broken World* (Grand Rapids, MI: Grace Publications, 2019), p. 124.

QUESTION 2: CURRENT CIRCUMSTANCES

How does knowing you are an ambassador for Christ motivate you to represent Him in your words, actions, and relationships?

_____

_____

_____

QUESTION 3: FUTURE PLANS - KNOWING THIS TRUTH

How can you intentionally share Christ's message of reconciliation with someone in your life this week?

_____

_____

_____

A Prayer of Gratitude for Being an Ambassador for Christ

Heavenly Father,

Thank You for entrusting me with the role of ambassador for Christ. I am humbled by the privilege of representing Him and sharing Your message of reconciliation with the world. Help me to reflect Christ's heart in all I do, bringing glory to You.

Teach me to speak and act with love, grace, and boldness, pointing others to the transformative power of Your salvation. May my life be a living testimony of Your mercy and truth.

In Jesus's Name,
Amen.

35. You Are Part of God's Family and Household

Scripture

Ephesians 2:19 "Consequently, you are no longer foreigners and strangers, but fellow citizens with God's people and also members of his household." (NIV)

Highlights

- **Transformational Truth:** At the moment of salvation, you are made members of God's family and His household, enjoying intimate fellowship and belonging with Him and His people.
- **Foundational Word:** "Household" (Greek: *oikeios*) signifies being part of a family or domestic circle.
- **Theological Insight:** J.I. Packer notes, "Adoption into God's household signifies the most profound relationship a [the] believer can have with God—a loving Father to His children."[36]

Grace Power-Up: Made a Member of God's Family and Household

QUESTION 1: EXAMINING GOD'S CHARACTER

How would your sense of identity and belonging change if God had **not** welcomed you into His family and household, leaving you as a stranger?

___

___

___

---

[36] J.I. Packer, *Knowing God* (Downers Grove, IL: InterVarsity Press, 1973), p. 207.

QUESTION 2: CURRENT CIRCUMSTANCES

How does knowing you are part of God's family and household bring comfort and reassurance during times of loneliness or rejection?

_____

_____

_____

QUESTION 3: FUTURE PLANS - KNOWING THIS TRUTH

How can you embrace your role as a member of God's family, fostering unity and love within His household?

_____

_____

_____

A Prayer of Gratitude for Being Made a Member of God's Family

Heavenly Father,

Thank You for welcoming me into Your family and household through salvation. I am overwhelmed by the privilege of belonging to You and enjoying intimate fellowship with You and Your people. Help me to live in the confidence and joy of being part of Your family.

Teach me to reflect Your love within the household of faith, promoting unity and caring for my brothers and sisters in Christ. May my life honor You and draw others into the joy of belonging to Your eternal family.

In Jesus's Name,
Amen.

The Believer's Future Hope

36. Your Future with Christ Is Guaranteed

Scripture

Romans 8:38-39 "For I am convinced that neither death nor life, neither angels nor demons, neither the present nor the future, nor any powers, neither height nor depth, nor anything else in all creation, will be able to separate us from the love of God that is in Christ Jesus our Lord." (NIV)

Highlights

- **Transformational Truth:** At the moment of salvation, you are guaranteed/assured of an eternal future with Christ, secured by His unchanging promises.
- **Foundational Word:** "Guaranteed" (*Greek: arrabōn*) refers to a pledge or down payment, ensuring the full and final fulfillment of a promise.
- **Theological Insight:** Dr. Sam Vinton, Jr. says, "Our future with Christ is guaranteed by the faithfulness of God, who has promised that nothing can separate us from His love or His eternal plan for us."[37]

Grace Power-Up: A Future with Christ That Is Guaranteed

QUESTION 1: EXAMINING GOD'S CHARACTER

Where would your hope and security lie if God had **not** guaranteed your eternal future with Christ, leaving you uncertain about your destiny?

_____

_____

_____

---

[37] Sam Vinton, Jr., *Eternal Security: Resting in God's Faithfulness* (Grand Rapids, MI: Grace Publications, 2008), p. 134.

QUESTION 2: CURRENT CIRCUMSTANCES

How does knowing your future with Christ is guaranteed, bring you peace and courage when facing trials or uncertainties in life?

_____

_____

_____

QUESTION 3: FUTURE PLANS - KNOWING THIS TRUTH

How can you live confidently and purposefully today, knowing your eternal future with Christ is secure?

_____

_____

_____

A Prayer of Gratitude for a Guaranteed Future with Christ

Heavenly Father,

Thank You for guaranteeing my eternal future with Christ. I am deeply grateful for Your unchanging promises that nothing can separate me from Your love. Help me to live in the peace and joy of this assurance, trusting in Your faithfulness no matter what I face.

Teach me to live confidently and purposefully, reflecting the hope of my secure future to others. May my life glorify You and draw others to the joy and security found in Your love.

In Jesus's Name, Amen.

37. You Are Promised an Eternal Inheritance

Scripture

Colossians 1:12 "And giving joyful thanks to the Father, who has qualified you to share in the inheritance of his holy people in the kingdom of light." (NIV)

Colossians 3:24 "Since you know that you will receive an inheritance from the Lord as a reward. It is the Lord Christ you are serving." (NIV)

Hebrews 9:15 "For this reason Christ is the mediator of a new covenant, that those who are called may receive the promised eternal inheritance—now that he has died as a ransom to set them free from the sins committed under the first covenant." (NIV)

Highlights

- **Transformational Truth:** At the moment of salvation, you receive an imperishable inheritance, kept in heaven, that cannot fade or be revoked, reflecting the eternal security of God's promise.

- **Foundational Word:** "Inheritance" (Greek: *klēronomia*) signifies a permanent and incorruptible possession.

- **Theological Insight**: Matthew Henry explains, "This inheritance is reserved in heaven for believers, untouchable by time or circumstance, assured by God's eternal decree."[38]

Grace Power-Up: Given an Inheritance

QUESTION 1: EXAMINING GOD'S CHARACTER

How would your trust in God's promises be affected if your inheritance in Christ could perish, spoil, or fade, leaving you uncertain of its permanence?

---

[38] Matthew Henry, *Matthew Henry's Commentary on the Whole Bible,* commentary on 1 Peter 1:4.

QUESTION 2: CURRENT CIRCUMSTANCES

How does knowing your inheritance in heaven is secure and imperishable give you encouragement, especially during times of loss or uncertainty? (Read 1 Peter 1:4)

QUESTION 3: FUTURE PLANS - KNOWING THIS TRUTH

How can you live with confidence and gratitude, focusing on your eternal inheritance and inspiring others to trust in God's unchanging promises?

A Prayer of Gratitude for an Inheritance

Heavenly Father,

Thank You for giving me an inheritance in Christ that is imperishable, unspoiled, and unfading. I am humbled by the security and permanence of Your promise, knowing that my future is firmly kept in Your hands.

Help me to live with peace and confidence, trusting in Your unchanging love and grace. May my life reflect the joy of this eternal inheritance, pointing others to the hope and assurance found in Christ.

In Jesus's Name,
Amen.

38. You Are Spiritually Glorified and Await Full Glorification

Scripture

Romans 8:30 "And those he predestined, he also called; those he called, he also justified; those he justified, he also glorified." (NIV)

Highlights

- **Transformational Truth:** At the moment of salvation, you are spiritually glorified in Christ, and you await complete glorification in eternity when you will share fully in Christ's glory.

- **Foundational Word:** "Glorified" (Greek: *doxazō*) means to be honored or made radiant, reflecting God's glory.

- **Theological Insight:** John Piper writes, "The glorification of the believer begins now in the transformation of their spirit and will be consummated in their resurrection bodies at Christ's return."[39]

Grace Power-Up: Glorified Spiritually and Awaiting Complete Glorification

QUESTION 1: EXAMINING GOD'S CHARACTER

How would your hope for eternity and your spiritual transformation be affected if God had **not** begun the work of glorifying you in Christ?

_____

_____

_____

[39] John Piper, *Future Grace: The Purifying Power of the Promises of God* (Colorado Springs, CO: Multnomah, 1995), p. 234.

QUESTION 2: CURRENT CIRCUMSTANCES

How does knowing you are spiritually glorified now and will be fully glorified in eternity encourage you to persevere through trials and struggles?

_____

_____

_____

QUESTION 3: FUTURE PLANS - KNOWING THIS TRUTH

How can you live each day with the hope and purpose of reflecting Christ's glory, even as you await the fullness of glorification?

_____

_____

_____

A Prayer of Gratitude for Spiritual Glorification

Heavenly Father,

Thank You for beginning the work of glorification in me through Christ and for the promise of complete glorification in eternity. I am humbled by Your grace that transforms me now and assures me of sharing in Christ's glory forever. Help me to live with this hope in every moment.

Teach me to persevere through trials, reflecting Your glory in my life and pointing others to the joy and promise of eternal life with You. May my life be a testimony to Your transforming power and faithfulness.

In Jesus's Name,
Amen.

39. You Were Given the Gift of God—Eternal Life

Scripture

Romans 6:23 "For the wages of sin is death, but the gift of God is eternal life in Christ Jesus our Lord." (NIV)

Highlights

- **Transformational Truth:** At the moment of salvation, God grants you His gift—eternal life through Jesus Christ. This gift, freely given by grace, contrasts the deserved wages of sin and secures your future with Him forever.

- **Foundational Word:** "Gift" (Greek: *charisma*) refers to a favor or blessing freely bestowed, without expectation of repayment. It emphasizes the unmerited, gracious nature of God's offer of eternal life.

- **Theological Insight:** John MacArthur states, "Eternal life is not earned but given as a gift to those who trust in Christ. It's the ultimate expression of God's grace—an unearned, undeserved blessing that secures our hope in Him."[40]

Grace Power-Up: The Gift of Eternal Life

QUESTION 1: EXAMINING GOD'S CHARACTER

What does the contrast between the wages of sin and the gift of God reveal about His grace and mercy?

___

___

---

[40] MacArthur, John, *The Gospel According to Jesus: What Does Jesus Mean When He Says 'Follow Me'?* Zondervan, Grand Rapids, MI (1994). p. 104.

QUESTION 2: CURRENT CIRCUMSTANCES

How does knowing you have the gift of eternal life impact the way you face life's uncertainties and challenges?

___

___

___

QUESTION 3: FUTURE PLANS - KNOWING THIS TRUTH

How can you live with a greater sense of purpose and urgency to share God's gift of eternal life with others?

___

___

___

A Prayer of Gratitude for the Gift of Eternal Life

Heavenly Father, thank You for the incredible gift of eternal life, given to me freely through Your grace and mercy. I am humbled and overwhelmed by the love that led You to offer salvation through Jesus Christ.

Help me to live each day in gratitude for this gift, seeking to honor You with my life. Teach me to share this hope with others, so they too may experience the joy of eternal life in Christ.

Thank You for transforming my destiny from death to life and for the assurance that I will dwell with You forever.

In Jesus's Name,

Amen.

40. Your Conscience Is Cleansed by Christ

Scripture

Hebrews 9:14 "How much more, then, will the blood of Christ, who through the eternal Spirit offered himself unblemished to God, cleanse our consciences from acts that lead to death, so that we may serve the living God!." (NIV)

Highlights

- **Transformational Truth:** At the moment of salvation, God cleanses your conscience from sin, enabling true worship.
- **Foundational Word:** "Cleansed" (Greek: *katharizo*) means to purify.
- **Theological Insight**: John Owen: "The blood of Christ purifies our conscience, liberating us to serve the living God."[41]

Grace Power-Up: Cleansing of the Conscience

QUESTION 1: EXAMINING GOD'S CHARACTER

How would your worship and service to God be affected if He had **not** cleansed your conscience from sin through the blood of Christ?

_____

_____

_____

---

[41] John Owen, *The Works of John Owen, Vol. 6: The Doctrine of the Saints' Perseverance Explained and Confirmed* (Edinburgh: Banner of Truth Trust, 1967), p. 305.

QUESTION 2: CURRENT CIRCUMSTANCES

How does knowing your conscience has been purified by Christ help you let go of guilt and approach God with confidence in worship?

_____

_____

_____

QUESTION 3: FUTURE PLANS - KNOWING THIS TRUTH

How can you live with a clear conscience, fully devoted to serving and glorifying the living God in your daily life?

_____

_____

_____

A Prayer of Gratitude for Cleansing of the Conscience

Heavenly Father,

Thank You for cleansing my conscience through the blood of Christ. I am humbled by the freedom to worship and serve You without the burden of guilt. Help me to live in the confidence of this purification and to approach You with a sincere heart.

Teach me to reflect this cleansing in my actions and relationships, serving You with devotion and gratitude. May my life honor You and draw others to Your saving grace.

In Jesus's Name,
Amen.

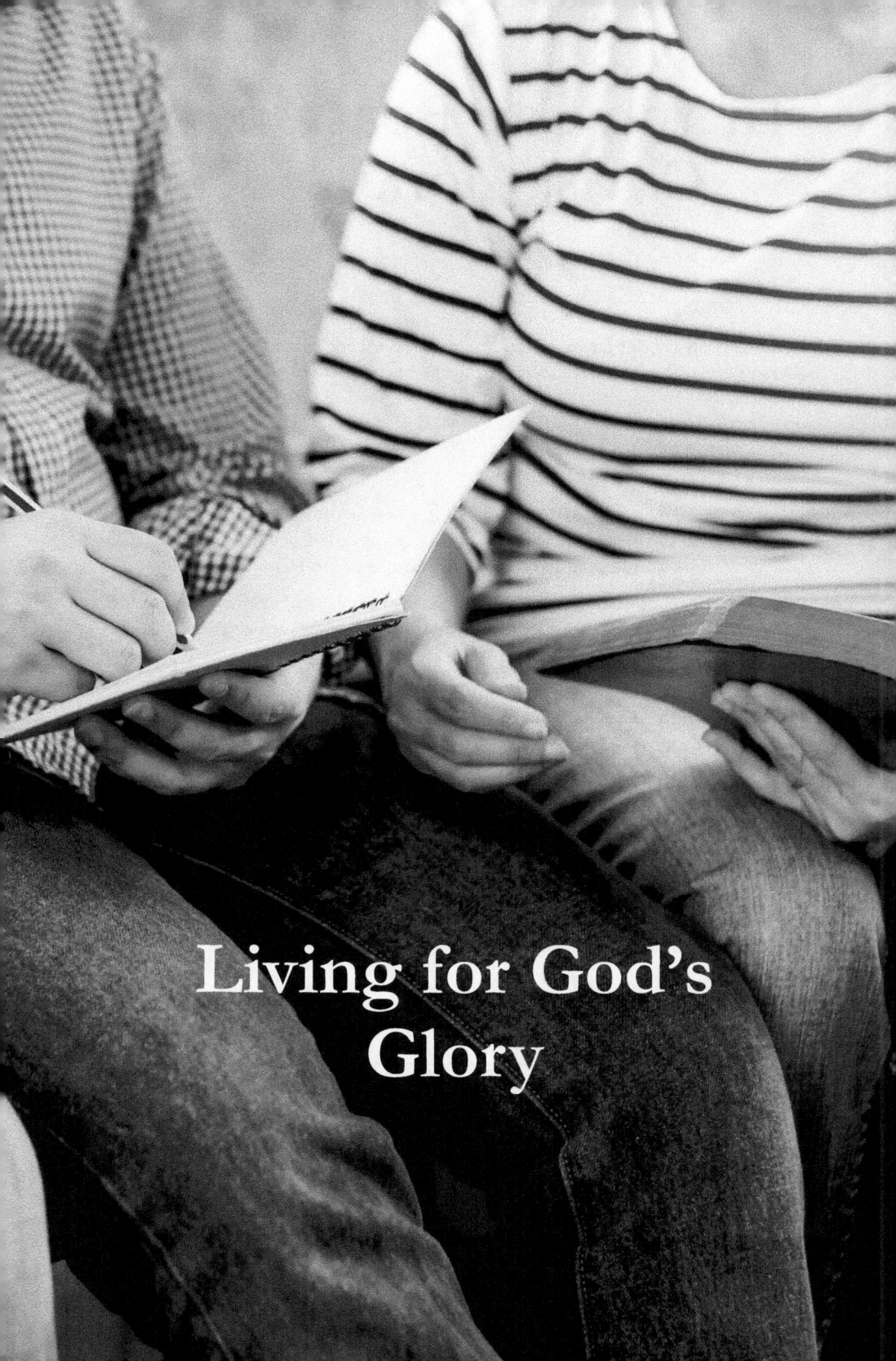

Living for God's Glory

41. You Can Boast in Christ Alone

Scripture

Galatians 6:14 "But far be it from me to boast except in the Cross of our Lord Jesus Christ, through which the world has been crucified to me, and I to the world." (NIV)

Highlights

- **Transformational Truth:** At the moment of salvation, the Cross of Jesus Christ becomes your only source of sufficiency in which to boast, as the world has been crucified to you and you to the world.
- **Foundational Word:** "Boast" (Greek: *kauchaomai*) conveys the act of exulting or rejoicing, redirected from human achievement to the redemptive work of Christ.
- **Theological Insight:** John Piper notes, "To boast in Christ is to magnify His sufficiency and humbly acknowledge our complete dependence on Him."[42]

Grace Power-Up: Boasting in Christ Alone

QUESTION 1: EXAMINING GOD'S CHARACTER

Where would your life and identity be rooted if Christ had **not** provided the sufficiency of His grace and salvation for you to boast in?

_____

_____

_____

---

[42] John Piper, *Desiring God: Meditations of a Christian Hedonist* (Colorado Springs, CO: Multnomah, 2003), p. 54.

QUESTION 2: CURRENT CIRCUMSTANCES

How does shifting your focus from your own achievements to boasting in Christ give you freedom from self-reliance and a servant heart?

_____

_____

_____

QUESTION 3: FUTURE PLANS - KNOWING THIS TRUTH

How can you actively magnify Christ in your daily life, making Him the center of your words and actions?

_____

_____

_____

A Prayer of Gratitude for Boasting in Christ Alone

Heavenly Father,

Thank You for giving me everything I need through the death, burial and resurrection of Christ from the cross. I recognize that my worth and strength come from Him alone. Teach me to let go of self-reliance and pride, boasting only in the sufficiency of Jesus.

Let my "knee-jerk" reaction be to boast in the Lord and not myself.

Help me to live each day magnifying His grace, showing others the joy and freedom found in depending on Him. May my life bring glory to You as I humbly acknowledge Christ as my all in all.

In Jesus's Name,

Amen.

42. You Are Redeemed by God

Scripture

Romans 3:24 "And all are justified freely by his grace through the redemption that came by Christ Jesus." (NIV)

Colossians 1:14 "In whom we have redemption, the forgiveness of sins." (NIV)

1 Peter 1:18 "For you know that it was not with perishable things such as silver or gold that you were redeemed from the empty way of life handed down to you from your ancestors." (NIV)

Highlights

- **Transformational Truth:** At the moment of salvation, you are redeemed by God, freed from the bondage of sin, and brought into a relationship with Him through the blood of Christ.
- **Foundational Word:** "Redeemed" (*Greek: apolytrōsis*) means to ransom, deliver, or set free by paying a price, emphasizing the cost of Christ's sacrifice for our freedom.
- **Theological Insight:** Erwin Lutzer shares, "We are redeemed not with perishable things, but through the infinite value of Christ's blood, securing our freedom and eternal life with God."[43]

Grace Power-Up: Redeemed by God

QUESTION 1: EXAMINING GOD'S CHARACTER

Where would you be if God had **not** redeemed you, leaving you enslaved to sin and separated from Him?

_____

_____

---

[43] Erwin W. Lutzer, *The Cross in the Shadow of the Crescent* (Eugene, OR: Harvest House Publishers, 2013), p. 78.

QUESTION 2: CURRENT CIRCUMSTANCES

How does knowing you are redeemed by the precious blood of Christ encourage you to live in freedom from guilt, shame, and sin?

_____

_____

_____

QUESTION 3: FUTURE PLANS - KNOWING THIS TRUTH

How can you honor God's costly redemption by living a life that reflects gratitude and devotion to Him?

_____

_____

_____

A Prayer of Gratitude for Being Redeemed by God

Heavenly Father,

Thank You for redeeming me through the precious blood of Jesus Christ. I am in awe of the sacrifice that set me free from the bondage of sin and brought me into a relationship with You. Help me to live in the freedom and joy of being redeemed, fully trusting in Your grace.

Teach me to honor Your sacrifice by living a life of gratitude, obedience, and devotion. May my life glorify You and draw others to the redemption found in Christ.

In Jesus's Name,
Amen.

43. You Are Buried with Christ

Scripture

Romans 6:4 "We were therefore buried with him through baptism into death in order that, just as Christ was raised from the dead through the glory of the Father, we too may live a new life." (NIV)

Colossians 2:12 "Having been buried with him in baptism, in which you were also raised with him through your faith in the working of God, who raised him from the dead." (NIV)

Highlights

- **Transformational Truth:** At the moment of salvation, you are spiritually buried with Christ, signifying the death of your old self and the beginning of a new life in Him.

- **Foundational Word:** "Buried" (*Greek: synthaptō*) means to be interred or laid to rest with, symbolizing unity with Christ in His death and the complete break from the power of sin.

- **Theological Insight**: Charles Baker shares, "Burial with Christ signifies the believer's complete identification with His death, leaving behind the old life dominated by sin and rising to walk in the newness of life."[44]

Grace Power-Up: Buried with Christ

QUESTION 1: EXAMINING GOD'S CHARACTER

Where would you remain if God had **not** buried your old self with Christ, leaving you enslaved to the power of sin and unable to walk in newness of life?

___

___

---

[44] Charles F. Baker, *A Dispensational Theology* (Grand Rapids, MI: Grace Bible College Publications, 1971), p. 421.

QUESTION 2: CURRENT CIRCUMSTANCES

How does knowing your old self has been buried with Christ empower you to break free from sin and embrace the new life He has given you?

QUESTION 3: FUTURE PLANS - KNOWING THIS TRUTH

How can you live each day as someone who has been raised with Christ, reflecting the newness of life in your actions and attitudes?

A Prayer of Gratitude for Being Buried with Christ

Heavenly Father, thank You for burying my old self with Christ, breaking the power of sin in my life and raising me to walk in newness of life. I am grateful for the transformation You have brought about through Your grace and love.

Teach me to live each day in the freedom of this truth, leaving behind my old ways, thoughts, habits and embracing the life You have called me to. May my actions and attitudes reflect the new life I have in Christ, bringing glory to You and pointing others to His redeeming work.

In Jesus's Name,

Amen.

44. You Are Saved by Grace

Scripture

Ephesians 2:8-9 "For it is by grace you have been saved, through faith—and this is not from yourselves, it is the gift of God—not by works, so that no one can boast." (NIV)

Highlights

- **Transformational Truth:** At the moment of salvation, you receive the free gift of salvation, which is entirely unearned and rooted solely in God's grace, not from your own works or merit.
- **Foundational Word:** "Grace" (Greek: *charis*) means unmerited favor or a free gift.
- **Theological Insight:** John Gowdy: "The beauty of grace lies in its unmerited nature, granting us salvation not by works, but as a divine gift that glorifies the giver, not the recipient."[45]

Grace Power-Up: Saved By Grace

QUESTION 1: EXAMINING GOD'S CHARACTER

How would your understanding of God's love and grace change if salvation were based on merit, leaving you to earn what only He can freely give?

_____

_____

_____

---

[45] John Gowdy, *Grace Unveiled: Understanding the Gift of Salvation* (Green Valley, AZ: Redemption Press, 2021), p. 76.

QUESTION 2: CURRENT CIRCUMSTANCES

How does knowing that salvation is a free gift of grace encourage you to rest in God's love and relinquish the pressure to earn His favor through works?

_____

_____

_____

QUESTION 3: FUTURE PLANS - KNOWING THIS TRUTH

How can you reflect the unmerited nature of God's grace by showing unconditional love and kindness to others, regardless of their actions or worthiness?

_____

_____

_____

A Prayer of Gratitude for being Saved by Grace

Heavenly Father,

Thank You for the incredible gift of salvation, given freely by Your grace alone and not by my works. I am humbled by the unmerited favor You have shown me and grateful that my salvation depends entirely on the Blood of Jesus Christ.

Help me to rest in the assurance of Your grace and to reflect it in my relationships and actions. Teach me to share the message of salvation with others, pointing them to the beauty of Your unearned and unconditional love.

In Jesus's Name,
Amen.

45. You Are Positioned in Christ

Scripture

2 Corinthians 5:17 "Therefore, if anyone is in Christ, the new creation has come: The old has gone, the new is here!." (NIV)

Highlights

- **Transformational Truth:** At the moment of salvation, you are united with Christ (placed "in Christ"), sharing in His life, righteousness, and inheritance.

- **Foundational Word:** "In Christ" (Greek: *en Christō*) signifies a spiritual union with Jesus, where the believer's identity and position are forever aligned with Him.

- **Theological Insight:** John MacArthur explains, "Being 'in Christ' means believers are spiritually connected to Him, sharing in His death, resurrection, and eternal life."[46]

Grace Power-Up: Placed "In Christ"

QUESTION 1: EXAMINING GOD'S CHARACTER

How would your life and identity be impacted if God had **not** placed you "in Christ", leaving you disconnected from His life and righteousness?

---

[46] John MacArthur, *The Believer's Life in Christ: Ephesians* (Chicago, IL: Moody Press, 1986), p. 37.

QUESTION 2: CURRENT CIRCUMSTANCES

How does knowing you are "in Christ" as a new creation help you face challenges, overcome sin, and embrace your true identity?

_____

_____

_____

QUESTION 3: FUTURE PLANS - KNOWING THIS TRUTH

How can you live each day as a reflection of your union with Christ, walking in His righteousness and purpose?

_____

_____

_____

A Prayer of Gratitude for Being Placed "In Christ"

Heavenly Father,

Thank You for uniting me with Christ, making me a new creation and aligning my life with His righteousness and inheritance. I am grateful that my identity is forever rooted in Him, and I no longer need to live in the old ways.

Teach me to embrace this truth daily, walking in the confidence and purpose of being "in Christ." Help me to reflect His life and love to those around me, glorifying You in all I do.

In Jesus's Name,
Amen.

Empowered by the Spirit

46. You Are Victorious over Darkness

Scripture

Colossians 2:15 "And having disarmed the powers and authorities, he made a public spectacle of them, triumphing over them by the cross." (NIV)

Highlights

- **Transformational Truth:** At the moment of salvation, you are made victorious over the powers of darkness through the triumph of Jesus Christ.

- **Foundational Word:** "Victor" (Greek: *nikaō*) means to conquer or overcome.

- **Theological Insight:** John MacArthur states, "Christ's victory over sin, death, and the forces of darkness is imputed to believers, granting them triumph in His name."[47]

Grace Power-Up: Victor over the Forces of Darkness

QUESTION 1: EXAMINING GOD'S CHARACTER

Where would you stand if God had **not** made you victorious through Christ, thereby leaving you defenseless against the powers of darkness?

_____

_____

_____

---

[47] John MacArthur, *The MacArthur New Testament Commentary: Romans 1-8* (Chicago, IL: Moody Publishers, 1991), p. 327.

QUESTION 2: CURRENT CIRCUMSTANCES

How does knowing Christ has triumphed over the powers of darkness encourage you to face spiritual battles with confidence and faith?

_____

_____

_____

QUESTION 3: FUTURE PLANS - KNOWING THIS TRUTH

How can you live each day as a victor, standing firm in Christ's triumph and resisting the influence of darkness?

_____

_____

_____

A Prayer of Gratitude for Victory over Darkness

Heavenly Father,

Thank You for granting me victory over the forces of darkness through Jesus Christ. I am grateful for the triumph of the cross, which disarmed sin, death, and spiritual powers. Help me to live each day in the confidence of this victory, relying on Your strength.

Teach me to stand firm in spiritual battles, reflecting Your power and bringing glory to Your name. May my life testify to the hope and freedom found in Christ's triumph.

In Jesus's Name,
Amen.

47. You Are Blessed with Every Spiritual Blessing

Scripture

Ephesians 1:3 "Praise be to the God and Father of our Lord Jesus Christ, who has blessed us in the heavenly realms with every spiritual blessing in Christ." (NIV)

Highlights

- **Transformational Truth:** At the moment of salvation, you are blessed with every spiritual blessing in Christ.

- **Foundational Word:** "Blessed" (Greek: *eulogeō*) means to be endowed with benefits or divine favor.

- **Theological Insight**: John Stott explains, "Every spiritual blessing in Christ is the sum of all that God has provided for the believer's spiritual growth, joy, and eternal security."[48]

Grace Power-Up: Blessed with Every Spiritual Blessing

QUESTION 1: EXAMINING GOD'S CHARACTER

How would your spiritual life and growth be limited if God had **not** blessed you with every spiritual blessing in Christ?

___

___

___

---

[48] John Stott, *The Message of Ephesians: God's New Society* (Downers Grove, IL: InterVarsity Press, 1979), p. 31.

QUESTION 2: CURRENT CIRCUMSTANCES

How does knowing you have access to every spiritual blessing encourage you to trust in God's provision and grace, even during challenging times?

_____

_____

_____

QUESTION 3: FUTURE PLANS - KNOWING THIS TRUTH

How can you intentionally live in the fullness of God's spiritual blessings, using them to grow in faith and serve others?

_____

_____

_____

A Prayer of Gratitude for Every Spiritual Blessing

Heavenly Father,

Thank You for blessing me with every spiritual blessing in Christ. I am overwhelmed by the richness of Your grace and the provision You have made for my spiritual growth, joy, and security. Help me to live in the fullness of these blessings, trusting in Your sufficiency.

Teach me to use these blessings to grow in faith, glorify You, and serve others with love and humility. May my life reflect the abundant grace You have so generously given me.

In Jesus's Name,
Amen.

48. You Are Complete in Christ

Scripture

Colossians 2:10 "And in Christ you have been brought to fullness. He is the head over every power and authority." (NIV)

Highlights

- **Transformational Truth:** At the moment of salvation, you are made complete in Christ, lacking nothing spiritually because of your union with Him.

- **Foundational Word:** "Complete" (Greek: *plēroō*) means to be filled or brought to fullness.

- **Theological Insight:** John MacArthur explains, "To be complete in Christ means that believers possess everything necessary for salvation, sanctification, and eternal life through Him."[49]

Grace Power-Up: Complete in Christ

QUESTION 1: EXAMINING GOD'S CHARACTER

How would your spiritual journey be different if God had **not** made you complete in Christ, leaving you lacking and unfulfilled?

---

[49] John MacArthur, *The MacArthur New Testament Commentary: Colossians and Philemon* (Chicago, IL: Moody Publishers, 1992), p. 104.

QUESTION 2: CURRENT CIRCUMSTANCES

How does knowing you are complete in Christ give you a sense of fulfillment?

_____

_____

_____

QUESTION 3: FUTURE PLANS - KNOWING THIS TRUTH

How can you live confidently in the fullness of Christ, using His sufficiency to grow in faith and serve others?

_____

_____

_____

A Prayer of Gratitude for Being Complete in Christ

Heavenly Father,

Thank You for making me complete in Christ, filling me with everything I need for salvation, sanctification, and eternal life. I am grateful for the sufficiency of Christ and the fullness I experience in Him. Help me to trust in this truth, especially when I feel inadequate.

Teach me to live confidently in Your provision, using the fullness of Christ to glorify You and serve others with humility and love. May my life reflect the completeness You have given me through Your grace.

In Jesus's Name,
Amen.

49. You Have Empowered Living through Christ

Scripture

Philippians 4:13 "I can do all things through him who strengthens me." (NIV)

Highlights

- **Transformational Truth:** At the moment of salvation, you are empowered to live victoriously through your union with Christ, relying on His strength, wisdom, and perseverance to overcome life's challenges.
- **Foundational Word:** "Strengthens" (Greek: *endynamoo*) means to empower or fill with strength.
- **Theological Insight:** John MacArthur explains, "Being in Christ enables believers to transcend their limitations and accomplish His purposes through divine empowerment."[50]

Grace Power-Up: Empowered Living through Christ

QUESTION 1: EXAMINING GOD'S CHARACTER

How would your approach to challenges be affected if God had **not** provided the empowering strength of Christ to enable you to live victoriously?

---

[50] John MacArthur, *The MacArthur New Testament Commentary:* Philippians (Chicago, IL: Moody Publishers, 2001), p. 166.

QUESTION 2: CURRENT CIRCUMSTANCES

How does knowing Christ strengthens you encourage you to face life's difficulties with confidence and rely on His power rather than your own?

_____

_____

_____

QUESTION 3: FUTURE PLANS - KNOWING THIS TRUTH

How can you intentionally depend on Christ's empowerment to fulfill His purposes in your life and overcome personal limitations?

_____

_____

_____

A Prayer of Gratitude for Empowered Living through Christ

Heavenly Father,

Thank You for empowering me through Christ to live victoriously and to overcome life's challenges. I am grateful for the strength, wisdom, and perseverance that come from being united with Him. Help me to rely on Your power instead of my own abilities in all circumstances.

Teach me to trust in Christ's strength daily, using it to fulfill Your purposes and to reflect Your glory. May my life demonstrate the joy and victory that come from living empowered by You.

In Jesus's Name,
Amen.

50. You Are Delivered from the Power of Darkness

Scripture

Colossians 1:13 "For he has rescued us from the dominion of darkness and brought us into the kingdom of the Son he loves." (NIV)

Highlights

- **Transformational Truth:** At the moment of salvation, you are rescued from the dominion and influence of darkness.
- **Foundational Word:** "Delivered" (Greek: *rhyomai*) means to rescue or draw to oneself, emphasizing God's act of liberation from spiritual bondage.
- **Theological Insight**: John MacArthur explains, "Deliverance from darkness signifies a complete rescue from the domain of sin and Satan, bringing believers into the light of Christ's rule."[51]

Grace Power-Up: Delivered from the Power of Darkness

QUESTION 1: EXAMINING GOD'S CHARACTER

How would your life and spiritual condition be different if God had **not** rescued you from the dominion of darkness and its influence?

_____

_____

_____

---

[51] John MacArthur, *The MacArthur New Testament Commentary: Colossians and Philemon* (Chicago, IL: Moody Publishers, 1992), p. 45.

QUESTION 2: CURRENT CIRCUMSTANCES

How does knowing you've been delivered from the power of darkness give you confidence and strength to resist temptation and walk in Christ's light?

_____

_____

_____

QUESTION 3: FUTURE PLANS - KNOWING THIS TRUTH

How can you live as someone freed from the power of darkness, reflecting Christ's light and leading others towards a saving knowledge of Christ?

_____

_____

_____

A Prayer of Gratitude for Deliverance from Darkness

Heavenly Father,

Thank You for rescuing me from the power of darkness and bringing me to Your beloved Son. I am humbled and grateful for Your act of being set me free from sin and Satan's dominion. Help me to walk confidently in the light of Christ.

Teach me to reflect His light in my actions, resisting the temptations of darkness and living as a testimony of Your grace. May my life point others to the freedom and joy found in You.

In Jesus's Name,
Amen.

Practical Faith

51. You Have a Heavenly Calling

Scripture

Philippians 3:14 "I press on toward the goal to win the prize for which God has called me heavenward in Christ Jesus." (NIV)

Highlights

- **Transformational Truth:** At the moment of salvation, you receive a heavenly calling, directing your lives toward God's eternal purpose and destiny in Christ.
- **Foundational Word:** "Calling" (Greek: *klēsis*) refers to a divine invitation to partake in God's eternal plan and glory.
- **Theological Insight:** John MacArthur states, "The heavenly calling elevates the believer's purpose, aligning their life with God's ultimate design for salvation and fellowship with Him."[52]

Grace Power-Up: A Heavenly Calling

QUESTION 1: EXAMINING GOD'S CHARACTER

Where would your life's purpose and direction be if God had **not** extended His heavenly calling to you, leaving you without an eternal hope?

_____

_____

_____

---

[52] John MacArthur, *The MacArthur New Testament Commentary: Hebrews* (Chicago, IL: Moody Publishers, 1983), p. 112.

QUESTION 2: CURRENT CIRCUMSTANCES

How does knowing you have a heavenly calling inspire you to persevere and stay focused on God's purpose during challenges or distractions?

___

___

___

QUESTION 3: FUTURE PLANS - KNOWING THIS TRUTH

How can you live intentionally, pressing toward the goal of your heavenly calling and fulfilling God's purpose for your life?

___

___

___

A Prayer of Gratitude for a Heavenly Calling

Heavenly Father,

Thank You for calling me heavenward in Christ Jesus, giving my life eternal purpose and direction. I am grateful for Your divine invitation to share in Your plan and glory. Help me to stay focused on this calling, even when challenges arise.

Teach me to live intentionally, pressing toward the goal You have set for me, and reflecting Your love and purpose in all I do. May my life glorify You and encourage others to embrace their heavenly calling.

In Jesus's Name,
Amen.

52. You Are Judged as Righteous, Moving from Guilt to Glory

Scripture

1 Corinthians 3:13-15 "Their work will be shown for what it is, because the Day will bring it to light. It will be revealed with fire, and the fire will test the quality of each person's work. If what has been built survives, the builder will receive a reward. If it is burned up, the builder will suffer loss but yet will be saved—even though only as one escaping through the flames." (NIV)

Highlights

- **Transformational Truth:** At the moment of salvation, you are no longer going to the "Great White Throne Judgment" for condemnation but you are instead destined for the "Bema Seat" Judgment, where all believers (including you) will receive rewards for your service to the Lord.

- **Foundational Word:** "Judgment" (Greek: *bēma*) refers to a platform or tribunal where rewards are distributed.

- **Theological Insight**: John MacArthur explains, "The Bema Seat Judgment is not a judgment of sin but an evaluation of believers' works to determine eternal rewards, as their sins have been fully paid for in Christ."[53]

Grace Power-Up: Moved from the Great White Throne Judgment to the Bema Seat Judgment

---

[53] John MacArthur, *The MacArthur New Testament Commentary: Romans 9-16* (Chicago, IL: Moody Publishers, 1994), p. 352.

QUESTION 1: EXAMINING GOD'S CHARACTER

How would your perspective on eternity change if God had **not** provided the Bema Seat Judgment, leaving you under the condemnation of the Great White Throne Judgment?

_____

_____

_____

QUESTION 2: CURRENT CIRCUMSTANCES

How does knowing your sins have been fully paid for in Christ and that you will stand before the Bema Seat Judgment encourage you to serve the Lord faithfully?

_____

_____

QUESTION 3: FUTURE PLANS - KNOWING THIS TRUTH

How can you live intentionally, focusing on building works that will endure and bring eternal rewards at the Bema Seat Judgment?

_____

_____

_____

A Prayer of Gratitude for Being Moved to the Bema Seat Judgment

Heavenly Father,

Thank You for saving me from the Great White Throne Judgment and securing my place at the Bema Seat Judgment. I am deeply grateful that my sins have been fully paid for by Christ and that You have given me the opportunity to serve You with an eternal purpose.

Help me to live intentionally, focusing on works that bring You glory and will endure for eternity. May my life reflect my gratitude and devotion, pointing others to the hope and assurance found in Christ. In Jesus's Name, Amen.

53. You Are Taught by God's Grace

Scripture

Titus 2:11-12 "For the grace of God has appeared that offers salvation to all people. It teaches us to say 'No' to ungodliness and worldly passions, and to live self-controlled, upright and godly lives in this present age." (NIV)

Highlights

- **Transformational Truth:** At the moment of salvation, the grace of God begins to teach and instruct you and guide you to live a godly life that reflects His righteousness.
- **Foundational Word:** "Instructs" (*Greek: paideuō*) means to train, educate, or discipline, emphasizing the transformative guidance of God's grace in the believer's life.
- **Theological Insight**: John Calvin writes, "The grace of God does not merely save; it instructs and trains us to renounce ungodliness and to pursue holiness in all aspects of life."[54]

Grace Power-Up: Taught by the Grace of God

QUESTION 1: EXAMINING GOD'S CHARACTER

How would your understanding of God's grace change if it did **not** guide and teach you to live a godly life, leaving you without direction or purpose?

_____

_____

_____

---

[54] John Calvin, *Institutes of the Christian Religion*, Book III, Chapter 6, Section 3 (Edinburgh: Calvin Translation Society, 1845).

QUESTION 2: CURRENT CIRCUMSTANCES

How is God's grace currently teaching you to say "No" to ungodliness and to live a self-controlled, upright, and godly life in your daily circumstances?

_____

_____

_____

QUESTION 3: FUTURE PLANS - KNOWING THIS TRUTH

How can you actively rely on God's grace to guide your decisions and actions, ensuring that your life increasingly reflects His righteousness?

_____

_____

_____

A Prayer of Gratitude for Being Taught by the Grace of God

Heavenly Father, thank You for the grace that not only saves but also instructs and guides me in living a life that honors You. I am grateful for Your constant presence and for teaching me to turn away from ungodliness and to pursue righteousness in every area of my life.

Help me to embrace the lessons of Your grace, living with self-control and godliness as I await the blessed hope of Christ's return. Teach me to rely on Your grace daily, trusting in Your Word and transforming power to shape my life for Your glory.

In Jesus's Name,

Amen.

54. You Are Given the Fruit of the Spirit

Scripture

Galatians 5:22-23 "But the fruit of the Spirit is love, joy, peace, forbearance, kindness, goodness, faithfulness, gentleness, and self-control. Against such things there is no law." (NIV)

Highlights

- **Transformational Truth:** At the moment of salvation, you receive the Spirit that produces His fruit, which manifests as godly characteristics and behaviors produced by the Holy Spirit in your life.
- **Foundational Word:** "Fruit" (Greek: *karpos*) signifies the visible outcome of the Holy Spirit's work in the believer's life.
- **Theological Insight:** John Stott explains, "The Fruit of the Spirit is evidence of the Spirit's transforming power, shaping the believer into Christlikeness."[55]

Grace Power-Up: Given the Fruit of the Spirit

QUESTION 1: EXAMINING GOD'S CHARACTER

How would your life reflect differently if God had **not** given you the Fruit of the Spirit, leaving you to rely solely on your human nature?

_____

_____

_____

---

[55] John Stott, *The Message of Galatians: Only One Way* (Downers Grove, IL: InterVarsity Press, 1968), p. 152

QUESTION 2: CURRENT CIRCUMSTANCES

How does recognizing the evidence of the Spirit's fruit in your life encourage you to grow in Christlikeness and respond with grace in difficult situations?

_____

_____

_____

QUESTION 3: FUTURE PLANS - KNOWING THIS TRUTH

How can you cultivate the Fruit of the Spirit intentionally, allowing God's character to shine through your actions and relationships?

_____

_____

_____

A Prayer of Gratitude for the Fruit of the Spirit

Heavenly Father,

Thank You for giving me Your Spirit that produces Fruit, which reflects Your transforming power in my life. I am grateful for the evidence of Your work in me through love, joy, peace, and the other godly characteristics You produce. Help me to rely on the Holy Spirit's guidance daily.

Teach me to cultivate these fruits intentionally, responding with grace in every situation and pointing others to Your goodness. May my life glorify You as a testimony to the Spirit's transforming power.

In Jesus's Name,
Amen.

55. You Will Be Rewarded for Labor in God's Service

Scripture

1 Corinthians 3:8 "The one who plants and the one who waters have one purpose, and they will each be rewarded according to their own labor." (NIV)

Highlights

- **Transformational Truth:** At the moment of salvation, you become co-laborers with God, and your faithful service will be rewarded according to your labor.
- **Foundational Word:** "Reward" (Greek: *misthos*) means compensation or wages, referring to the recognition and honor given for faithful work.
- **Theological Insight**: Charles Spurgeon states, "God graciously rewards what He Himself works in us, acknowledging our labor for His glory."[56]

Grace Power-Up: Receive a Reward for Labor in God's Service

QUESTION 1: EXAMINING GOD'S CHARACTER

How would your motivation to serve God change if He did **not** graciously reward faithful labor done for His glory?

_____

_____

_____

---

[56] Charles Spurgeon, *Metropolitan Tabernacle Pulpit*, Vol. 34, Sermon No. 2004: *The Reward of the Righteous* (London: Passmore and Alabaster, 1888), p. 428.

QUESTION 2: CURRENT CIRCUMSTANCES

How does knowing that your labor for God has eternal significance encourage you to persevere in serving Him, even when it feels unnoticed or challenging?

_____

_____

_____

QUESTION 3: FUTURE PLANS - KNOWING THIS TRUTH

How can you dedicate your efforts to serving God with joy and faithfulness, knowing that your work will be rewarded in His perfect timing?

_____

_____

_____

A Prayer of Gratitude for Rewards in God's Service

Heavenly Father,

Thank You for the privilege of being a co-laborer in the Body of Christ and for the promise of rewards for faithful service. I am humbled by Your grace that acknowledges and honors the work You accomplish through me. Help me to serve You with joy, faithfulness, and perseverance.

Teach me to focus on eternal rewards, dedicating my efforts to Your glory and trusting in Your perfect timing. May my life be a testimony to the joy and fulfillment found in laboring for You.

In Jesus's Name,
Amen.

Unity and Service in the Body of Christ

56. You Have the Privilege to Run Life's Race with Christ

Scripture

2 Timothy 4:7 "I have fought the good fight, I have finished the race, I have kept the faith." (NIV)

1 Corinthians 9:24-27 "Do you not know that in a race all the runners run, but only one gets the prize? Run in such a way as to get the prize. Everyone who competes in the games goes into strict training. They do it to get a crown that will not last, but we do it to get a crown that will last forever. Therefore I do not run like someone running aimlessly; I do not fight like a boxer beating the air. No, I strike a blow to my body and make it my slave so that after I have preached to others, I myself will not be disqualified for the prize." (NIV)

Highlights

- **Transformational Truth:** At the moment of salvation, you are called to run the race of faith alongside Christ, striving for the eternal prize through perseverance and discipline.

- **Foundational Word:** "Run" (Greek: *trechō*) signifies active participation and effort in pursuing God's purpose.

- **Theological Insight**: John MacArthur explains, "The Christian life is like a race—demanding endurance, discipline, and focus, with Christ as our ultimate prize and example."[57]

---

[57] John MacArthur, *The MacArthur New Testament Commentary: Hebrews* (Chicago, IL: Moody Publishers, 1983), p. 409.

Grace Power-Up: Privilege to Run the Race with Christ

QUESTION 1: EXAMINING GOD'S CHARACTER

How would your journey of faith differ if God had **not** invited you to run the race with Christ, leaving you without direction or purpose?

___

___

QUESTION 2: CURRENT CIRCUMSTANCES

How does knowing Christ runs the race alongside you give you strength and encouragement when the path feels difficult or overwhelming?

___

___

QUESTION 3: FUTURE PLANS - KNOWING THIS TRUTH

How can you train spiritually and run with perseverance, keeping your focus on Christ and the eternal prize He promises?

___

___

A Prayer of Gratitude for the Privilege to Run the Race with Christ

Heavenly Father,

Thank You for calling me to run the race of faith with Christ as my example and prize. I am grateful for the purpose, endurance, and joy You provide as I strive to follow Your will. Help me to run with discipline, perseverance, and unwavering focus on You.

Teach me to rely on Christ's strength and to train my heart and mind for the journey ahead. May my life glorify You as I press on toward the eternal crown that will never fade. In Jesus's Name, Amen.

57. You Are Rewarded for Diligently Seeking God

Scripture

Hebrews 11:6 "And without faith it is impossible to please God, because anyone who comes to him must believe that he exists and that he rewards those who earnestly seek him." (NIV)

Highlights

- **Transformational Truth:** At the moment of salvation, God rewards you for earnestly seeking Him in faith, affirming His faithfulness to those who trust in Him.

- **Foundational Word:** "Rewarder" (Greek: *misthapodotēs*) means one who pays or compensates, emphasizing God's promise to respond to faith with blessings.

- **Theological Insight:** Charles Spurgeon explains, "God delights in faith and rewards it, not because it earns His favor, but because it honors Him as trustworthy."[58]

Grace Power-Up: God is the Rewarder of Those Who Diligently Seek Him

QUESTION 1: EXAMINING GOD'S CHARACTER

What would your faith journey look like if God did **not** reward you for diligently seeking Him, leaving you without assurance of His response to your faith?

_____

_____

_____

---

[58] Charles Spurgeon, *Metropolitan Tabernacle Pulpit*, Vol. 36, Sermon No. 2132: *Faith's Reward* (London: Passmore and Alabaster, 1890), p. 467.

QUESTION 2: CURRENT CIRCUMSTANCES

How does knowing that God rewards your earnest pursuit of Him encourage you to trust and seek Him more deeply, even in challenging seasons?

_____

_____

_____

QUESTION 3: FUTURE PLANS - KNOWING THIS TRUTH

How can you commit to seeking God diligently, trusting in His faithfulness to reward your faith and devotion?

_____

_____

_____

A Prayer of Gratitude for God is the Rewarder

Heavenly Father,

Thank You for being a faithful rewarder of those who diligently seek You. I am grateful for the assurance that Your gift of faith is not in vain and that You delight in responding to my trust and pursuit of You. Help me to seek You earnestly and consistently, no matter the circumstances and not matter the results. Knowing I can trust You even when I may never see the rewards in my earthly life.

Teach me to rely on Your faithfulness and to honor You through my devotion and obedience. May my life reflect the joy and peace that come from trusting in Your promises.

In Jesus's Name,

Amen.

58. You Can Trust in God Rather than Human Wisdom

Scripture

1 Corinthians 2:5 "So that your faith might not rest on human wisdom, but on God's power." (NIV)

Highlights

- **Transformational Truth:** At the moment of salvation, you are given the privilege and honor to place your complete trust in God, who is faithful, sovereign, and all-wise, instead of relying on the fallible and uncertain wisdom of man.
- **Foundational Word:** "Trust" (Greek: *pepoithēsis*) refers to confident reliance or assurance in God's character and promises.
- **Theological Insight:** Charles Spurgeon writes, "To trust in God rather than man is to rest in the infinite wisdom and power of the Creator, who never fails His people."[59]

Grace Power-Up: Trusting in God Rather than the Wisdom of Man

QUESTION 1: EXAMINING GOD'S CHARACTER

How would your life and decisions be different if God had **not** given you the ability to trust in His perfect wisdom, leaving you to rely solely on the limited and uncertain wisdom of man?

_____

_____

_____

---

[59] Charles Spurgeon, *Metropolitan Tabernacle Pulpit*, Vol. 27, Sermon No. 1605: *Trust in God Alone* (London: Passmore and Alabaster, 1881), p. 362.

QUESTION 2: CURRENT CIRCUMSTANCES

How does trusting in God's Word instead of human wisdom bring clarity when facing difficult decisions or challenges?

_____

_____

_____

QUESTION 3: FUTURE PLANS - KNOWING THIS TRUTH

How can you actively demonstrate trust in God's Word and power in your decisions and actions this week?

_____

_____

_____

A Prayer of Gratitude for Trusting in God

Heavenly Father,

Thank You for giving me the privilege of trusting in Your infinite wisdom and power rather than the fallible wisdom of man. I am grateful for the peace and clarity that come from resting in Your care. Help me to rely on You fully, especially in moments of uncertainty.

Teach me to desire Your Word and seek Your guidance and to act in faith, knowing that Your plans are always perfect. May my life reflect the confidence and assurance found in trusting You above all else.

In Jesus's Name,

Amen.

59. You Are Called to Be Known for Your Faith

Scripture

1 Thessalonians 1:8 "The Lord's message rang out from you not only in Macedonia and Achaia—your faith in God has become known everywhere. Therefore we do not need to say anything about it." (NIV)

2 Thessalonians 1:3-4 "We ought always to thank God for you, brothers and sisters, and rightly so, because your faith is growing more and more, and the love all of you have for one another is increasing. Therefore, among God's churches we boast about your perseverance and faith in all the persecutions and trials you are enduring." (NIV)

Highlights

- **Transformational Truth:** At the moment of salvation, you are given the example and call to live in such a way that your faith becomes known and celebrated, inspiring others to trust in Christ.

- **Foundational Word:** "Notorious" (Greek: *logos*) implied through reputation) conveys the idea of being widely known for faith and works.

- **Theological Insight:** John MacArthur states, "The Thessalonian believers lived out their faith so vibrantly that they became a model for others, demonstrating what it means to trust and follow Christ fully."[60]

Grace Power-Up: Called to Be Notorious for Our Faith

QUESTION 1: EXAMINING GOD'S CHARACTER

How would your faith journey differ if God had **not** empowered you to live a vibrant and visible faith that inspires others?

---

[60] John MacArthur, *The MacArthur New Testament Commentary: 1 & 2 Thessalonians* (Chicago, IL: Moody Publishers, 2002), p. 28.

QUESTION 2: CURRENT CIRCUMSTANCES

How does knowing that your faith can impact others motivate you to live boldly and authentically for Christ in your daily life?

QUESTION 3: FUTURE PLANS - KNOWING THIS TRUTH

How can you intentionally share your faith and let it "ring out" in ways that draw others to trust and follow Christ?

A Prayer of Gratitude for Being Called to Be Notorious for Faith

Heavenly Father,

Thank You for calling me to live a faith that is vibrant, visible, and inspiring to others. I am grateful for the example of fellow believers who boldly trust in You and reflect Your glory. Help me to follow their lead and live in a way that honors You.

Teach me to share my faith with boldness and love, allowing Your message and Your Word to "ring out" through my life. May my actions and words point others to the hope and joy found in Christ.

In Jesus's Name,
Amen.

60. You Have Spiritual Fathers and Leaders to Imitate

Scripture

1 Thessalonians 1:6 "You became imitators of us and of the Lord, for you welcomed the message in the midst of severe suffering with the joy given by the Holy Spirit." (NIV)

Highlights

- **Transformational Truth:** At the moment of salvation, you are blessed with the example of spiritual fathers and leaders, like Paul and other faithful believers, to guide and inspire others in their walk with Christ.

- **Foundational Word:** "Imitate" (Greek: *mimētēs*) means to follow or emulate the actions, faith, and character of godly examples.

- **Theological Insight:** John Stott explains, "Godly leaders, by their lives and teaching, provide a model for believers to imitate as they grow in faith and service."[61]

Grace Power-Up: Honored with Examples of Spiritual Fathers and Leaders to Imitate

QUESTION 1: EXAMINING GOD'S CHARACTER

How would your spiritual growth and understanding be affected if God had **not** provided godly leaders and examples to guide and inspire you in your faith journey?

---

[61] John Stott, *The Message of 1 Timothy and Titus: The Life of the Local Church* (Downers Grove, IL: InterVarsity Press, 1996), p. 102.

QUESTION 2: CURRENT CIRCUMSTANCES

How does having faithful leaders and spiritual mentors to imitate encourage you to persevere in your faith, even in challenging times? (Read 2 Timothy 2:2, How many spiritual fathers can you count?)

_____

_____

_____

QUESTION 3: FUTURE PLANS - KNOWING THIS TRUTH

How can you follow the example of godly leaders in your own walk and become a model for others to imitate in their faith?

_____

_____

_____

A Prayer of Gratitude for Spiritual Leaders to Imitate

Heavenly Father,

Thank You for providing godly leaders and spiritual mentors who inspire and guide me in my faith journey. I am grateful for their example of steadfast faith and joy in the midst of trials. Help me to learn from their lives and to grow in Christlikeness as I follow their lead.

Teach me to reflect their godly example in my own life, becoming a source of encouragement and inspiration for others. May my faith and actions honor You and point others to Your love and truth.

In Jesus's Name,

Amen.

God's Grace and Provision

61. You Welcome the Good News with Joy

Scripture

1 Thessalonians 1:6 "You became imitators of us and of the Lord, for you welcomed the message in the midst of severe suffering with the joy given by the Holy Spirit." (NIV)

Highlights

- **Transformational Truth:** At the moment of salvation, you are given the privilege of receiving the Gospel of Jesus Christ with great joy, even in the midst of trials and challenges.
- **Foundational Word:** "Welcome" (Greek: *dechomai*) means to receive or accept gladly.
- **Theological Insight:** John MacArthur explains, "The joy of receiving the Gospel transcends circumstances, as it is rooted in the eternal hope and promises of Christ."[62]

Grace Power-Up: Privilege to Welcome the Good News with Joy

QUESTION 1: EXAMINING GOD'S CHARACTER

How would your life and perspective on trials differ if God had **not** given you the privilege of welcoming the Gospel with joy, leaving you without hope in challenging circumstances?

_____

_____

_____

---

[62] John MacArthur, *The MacArthur New Testament Commentary: Philippians* (Chicago, IL: Moody Publishers, 2001), p. 47.

QUESTION 2: CURRENT CIRCUMSTANCES

How does the joy of the Gospel help you navigate suffering or hardships, knowing that your hope is rooted in Christ's eternal promises? (Consider: Are joy and happiness the same?)

QUESTION 3: FUTURE PLANS - KNOWING THIS TRUTH

How can you share the joy of the Gospel with others, especially those who are facing difficulties, so they too may experience its transformative power?

A Prayer of Gratitude for Welcoming the Good News with Joy

Heavenly Father,

Thank You for giving me the privilege to receive the Gospel with joy, even in the midst of trials. I am deeply grateful for the eternal hope and promises found in Christ that transcend my circumstances. Help me to hold onto this joy and let it shape my attitude and actions daily.

Teach me to share the good news with others, spreading the hope and joy of salvation to those who need it most. May my life reflect the peace and assurance that comes from knowing and trusting You.

In Jesus's Name,
Amen.

62. You Are Partakers of Christ

Scripture

Philippians 3:10 "I want to know Christ—yes, to know the power of his resurrection and participation in his sufferings, becoming like him in his death." (NIV)

2 Peter 1:4 "Through these he has given us his very great and precious promises, so that through them you may participate in the divine nature, having escaped the corruption in the world caused by evil desires." (NIV)

Hebrews 3:14 "We have come to share [Partakers] in Christ, if indeed we hold our original conviction firmly to the very end." (NIV)

Highlights

- **Transformational Truth:** At the moment of salvation, you become partakers of Christ—sharing in His divine nature, His sufferings, and ultimately His glory. This profound union transforms your identity and purpose.
- **Foundational Word:** "Partakers" (Greek: *metochos*) means to share in or participate, emphasizing an active and intimate involvement in Christ's life, nature, and mission.
- **Theological Insight:** John Owen states, "To partake of Christ is to embrace all that He is—His sufferings, resurrection, and glory—through faith, enabling us to grow into His likeness and live for His purposes."[63]

Grace Power-Up: Partakers of Christ

---

[63] Owen, John, (1850). *The works of John Owen, Volume 6*. Edinburgh: Johnstone and Hunter. (1850). p. 352.

QUESTION 1: EXAMINING GOD'S CHARACTER

How would your understanding of God's love and grace change if God had **not** invited you to partake in Christ's divine nature, leaving you without hope of transformation?

_____

_____

_____

QUESTION 2: CURRENT CIRCUMSTANCES

How does knowing you are a partaker of Christ's life and sufferings bring strength and encouragement during difficult times?

_____

_____

_____

QUESTION 3: FUTURE PLANS - KNOWING THIS TRUTH

How can you live out your role as a partaker of Christ, reflecting His divine nature and sharing His love in your daily life?

_____

_____

A Prayer of Gratitude for Being Partakers of Christ

Heavenly Father, thank You for making me a partaker of Christ—sharing in His divine nature and being united with Him in life, suffering, and glory. I am overwhelmed by the depth of Your grace and the privilege of being brought into such a close relationship with You.

Help me to live each day with the confidence and joy of knowing that I am united with Christ. Teach me to embrace both the power of His resurrection and the fellowship of His sufferings, trusting in Your purpose for my life.

In Jesus's Name, Amen.

63. You Are Honored to Serve and Suffer for the Gospel

Scripture

Philippians 1:29 "For it has been granted to you on behalf of Christ not only to believe in him, but also to suffer for him." (NIV)

2 Timothy 3:12 "In fact, everyone who wants to live a godly life in Christ Jesus will be persecuted." (NIV)

Highlights

- **Transformational Truth:** At the moment of salvation, you are called to the privilege of serving Christ and even considering it an honor to endure persecution for the sake of the Gospel.

- **Foundational Word:** "Persecuted" (Greek: *diōkō*) means to be pursued or harassed, often for one's faith.

- **Theological Insight:** Charles Spurgeon writes, "To suffer for Christ is not a penalty but a privilege, for it draws us nearer to Him and magnifies His name through our endurance."[64]

Grace Power-Up: Honored to Serve and Suffer for the Gospel

QUESTION 1: EXAMINING GOD'S CHARACTER

How would your perspective on faith and trials change if God had **not** called you to serve Him and given you the strength to view persecution as an honor for His name?

---

[64] Charles Spurgeon, *Metropolitan Tabernacle Pulpit*, Vol. 22, Sermon No. 1287: *The Joy of the Lord in Suffering* (London: Passmore and Alabaster, 1876), p. 497.

QUESTION 2: CURRENT CIRCUMSTANCES

How does knowing that suffering for Christ is a privilege encourage you to stand firm in your faith, even when facing opposition or hardship?

QUESTION 3: FUTURE PLANS - KNOWING THIS TRUTH

How can you boldly serve Christ and share the Gospel, trusting God to use your endurance to magnify His name and draw others to Him? (Read Romans 5:1-5)

A Prayer of Gratitude for Serving and Suffering for the Gospel

Heavenly Father,

Thank You for the privilege of serving Christ and for the honor of enduring persecution for His sake. I am humbled by the calling to magnify Your name through my faith and perseverance. Help me to stand firm in trials, by trusting in Your Word and Your strength and grace.

Teach me to embrace every opportunity to serve You boldly, knowing that even suffering for Your Gospel brings glory to Your name. May my life reflect the joy and hope found in serving You, inspiring others to trust in Your love and Your Word of truth.

In Jesus's Name, Amen.

64. You Can Be Confident that God Will Finish His Work in You

Scripture

Philippians 1:6 "Being confident of this, that he who began a good work in you will carry it on to completion until the day of Christ Jesus." (NIV)

Highlights

- **Transformational Truth:** At the moment of salvation, God starts a good work in you that He will carry on to completion, guaranteeing your ultimate sanctification and glorification.
- **Foundational Word:** "Completion" (*Greek: teleiōsis*) refers to the process of bringing something to its intended goal or perfect fulfillment.
- **Theological Insight:** John MacArthur states, "God's work in the believer is both certain and continuous, ensuring that His purpose in their life will reach its divine culmination."[65]

Grace Power-Up: Confident God Will Finish His Work in You

QUESTION 1: EXAMINING GOD'S CHARACTER

How would your journey of faith be impacted if God did **not** promise to complete the good work He began in you, leaving your growth and sanctification uncertain?

---

[65] John MacArthur, *The MacArthur New Testament Commentary: Philippians* (Chicago, IL: Moody Publishers, 2001), p. 41.

QUESTION 2: CURRENT CIRCUMSTANCES

How does knowing God is continuously working in your life give you peace and motivation to persevere, even when progress feels slow or difficult?

_____

_____

_____

QUESTION 3: FUTURE PLANS - KNOWING THIS TRUTH

How can you live with confidence and hope, trusting in God's promise to bring His work in you to its perfect completion?

_____

_____

_____

A Prayer of Gratitude for God's Promise to Finish His Good Work in You

Heavenly Father,

Thank You for the assurance that the good work You have begun in me will be carried to completion. I am grateful for Your faithfulness and Your continuous work in shaping me into Christ's image. Help me to trust in Your timing, Your Word and Your plan, even when I cannot see the full picture.

Teach me to live with confidence and perseverance, knowing that Your purpose for my life will reach its divine fulfillment. May my life reflect Your transforming power and encourage others to trust in Your faithfulness.

In Jesus's Name,

Amen.

65. You Have Full Access to God

Scripture

Ephesians 2:18 "For through him we both have access to the Father by one Spirit." (NIV)

Highlights

- **Transformational Truth:** At the moment of salvation, you are granted direct access to God through Jesus Christ.
- **Foundational Word:** "Access" (Greek: *prosagōgē*) signifies an introduction or approach to someone of high rank.
- **Theological Insight:** John Calvin states, "Through Christ, believers have access to the Father, a privilege once unattainable under the law but made possible by grace."[66]

Grace Power-Up: Access to God

QUESTION 1: EXAMINING GOD'S CHARACTER

How would your life and prayers be affected if God had **not** granted you direct access to Him through Jesus Christ or you lived under the Law and had to go through a Priest?

_____

_____

_____

---

[66] John Calvin, *Institutes of the Christian Religion*, Book III, Chapter 20, Section 3 (Edinburgh: Calvin Translation Society, 1845).

QUESTION 2: CURRENT CIRCUMSTANCES

How does having direct access to God give you peace and confidence when you need guidance, comfort, or strength?

_____

_____

_____

QUESTION 3: FUTURE PLANS - KNOWING THIS TRUTH

How can you intentionally approach God in prayer and dependence, deepening your relationship with Him in your daily life?

_____

_____

_____

A Prayer of Gratitude for Access to God

Heavenly Father,

Thank You for granting me direct access to You through Jesus Christ. I am humbled by the privilege of coming before You freely, knowing that You hear me and care for me. Help me to approach You with confidence, trusting in Your grace and love.

Teach me to rely on You in every aspect of my life, seeking Your Word, Your guidance, comfort, and strength. May my relationship with You grow deeper each day as I embrace the access You have so graciously provided.

In Jesus's Name,
Amen.

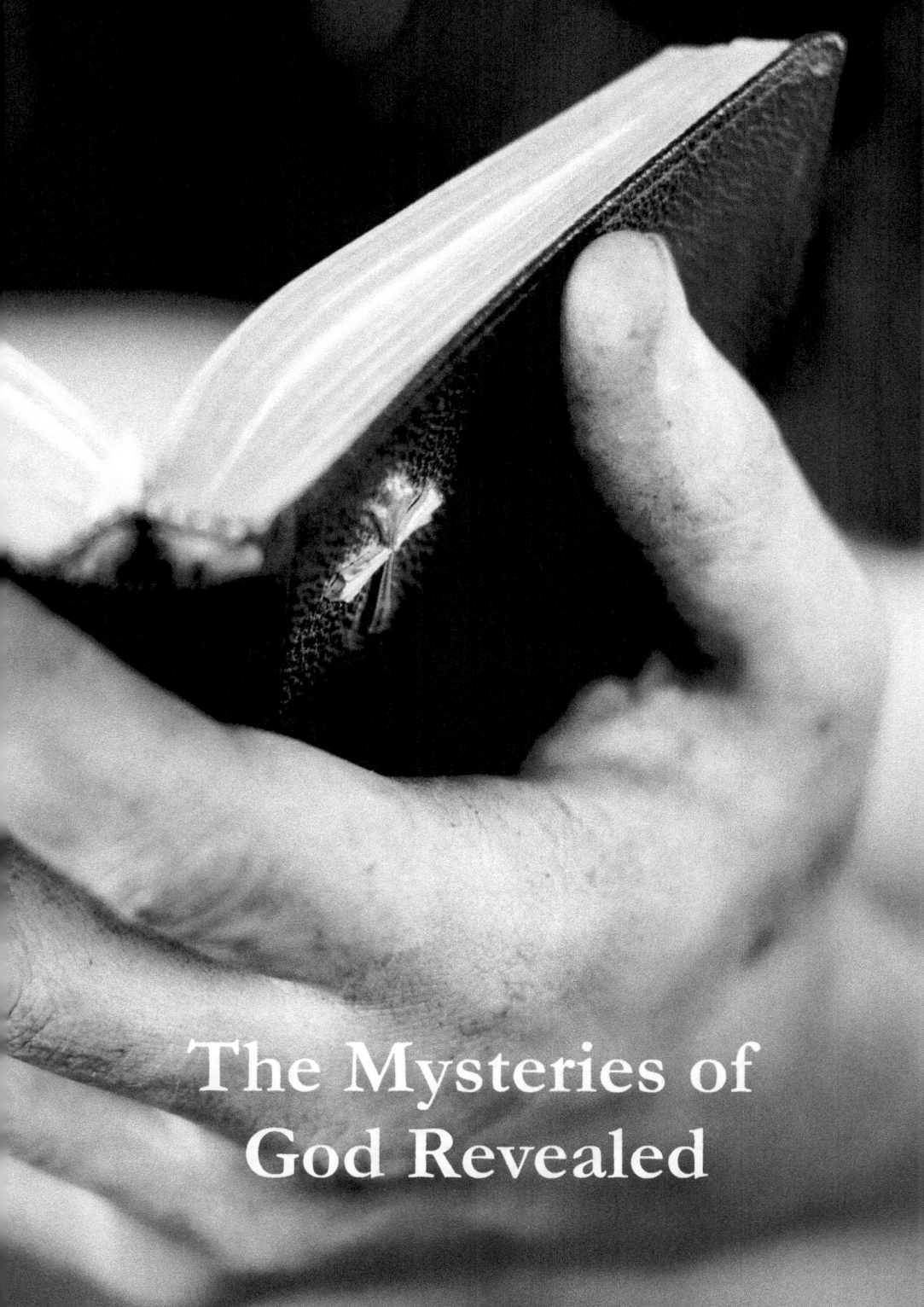

The Mysteries of God Revealed

66. You Find Grace and Mercy in Time of Need

Scripture

Hebrews 4:16 "Let us then approach God's throne of grace with confidence, so that we may receive mercy and find grace to help us in our time of need." (NIV)

Highlights

- **Transformational Truth:** At the moment of salvation, you are granted access to God's throne of grace, where you can confidently seek His mercy and find His grace in every time of need.
- **Foundational Word:** "Mercy" (Greek: *eleos*) signifies His compassion and help in times of weakness.
- **Theological Insight:** Charles Spurgeon notes, "God's throne of grace is always accessible, providing mercy for our failures and grace for our needs, all through Christ."[67]

Grace Power-Up: Find Grace and Mercy in Time of Need

QUESTION 1: EXAMINING GOD'S CHARACTER

How would your life and struggles be different if God's throne of grace were **not** accessible, leaving you without His mercy and help in times of need?

_____

_____

_____

---

[67] Charles Spurgeon, *Metropolitan Tabernacle Pulpit*, Vol. 31, Sermon No. 1848: *The Throne of Grace* (London: Passmore and Alabaster, 1885), p. 387.

QUESTION 2: CURRENT CIRCUMSTANCES

How does knowing you can approach God's throne of grace with confidence to receive grace and marcy, bring you peace and strength when facing challenges or failures?

_____

_____

_____

QUESTION 3: FUTURE PLANS - KNOWING THIS TRUTH

How can you cultivate a habit of seeking God's grace and mercy daily, relying on His provision to guide and sustain you?

_____

_____

_____

A Prayer of Gratitude for Grace and Mercy in Time of Need

Heavenly Father,

Thank You for giving me access to Your throne of grace, where I can confidently seek Your mercy and find help in every time of need. I am grateful for Your compassion and the grace You provide to sustain and strengthen me.

Teach me to read Your Word and approach You daily with confidence and humility, trusting in Your provision and faithfulness. May my life reflect the peace and hope found in relying on Your grace and mercy.

In Jesus's Name,
Amen.

67. You Are Part of the Mystery of the Body of Christ

Scripture

Ephesians 3:3-6 "That is, the mystery made known to me by revelation, as I have already written briefly. In reading this, then, you will be able to understand my insight into the mystery of Christ, which was not made known to people in other generations as it has now been revealed by the Spirit to God's holy apostles and prophets. This mystery is that through the gospel the Gentiles are heirs together with Israel, members together of one body, and sharers together in the promise in Christ Jesus." (NIV)

Highlights

- **Transformational Truth:** At the moment of salvation, you become a member of the revealed mystery of the Body of Christ, which unites Jews and Gentiles as one in Christ through faith, forming one spiritual family.
- **Foundational Word:** "Mystery" (Greek: *mysterion*) signifies a divine truth previously hidden but now disclosed through revelation.
- **Theological Insight:** Dr. Sam Vinton, Jr. explains, "The unity of Jew and Gentile in the Body of Christ is a testimony to the grace of God, a mystery hidden for ages but now revealed to show His plan for reconciliation through Christ."[68]

Grace Power-Up: Mystery of the Body of Christ Revealed

---

[68] Sam Vinton, Jr., *The Mystery of Christ and the Church* (Grand Rapids, MI: Grace Publications, 2008), p. 145.

QUESTION 1: EXAMINING GOD'S CHARACTER

How would your understanding of God's grace and unity be affected if the mystery of the Body of Christ, uniting Jew and Gentile, had **not** been revealed?

___

___

QUESTION 2: CURRENT CIRCUMSTANCES

How does knowing you are part of the unified Body of Christ encourage you to embrace and celebrate the diversity and fellowship within God's spiritual family?

___

___

QUESTION 3: FUTURE PLANS - KNOWING THIS TRUTH

How can you actively promote unity and love within the Body of Christ, reflecting the reconciliation and grace God has shown through Christ?

___

___

A Prayer of Gratitude for Revealing the Mystery of the Body of Christ

Heavenly Father,

Thank You for revealing the mystery of the Body of Christ, uniting all believers —Jew and Gentile—as one spiritual family. I am grateful for Your grace that reconciles us to You and to one another through Christ. Help me to live in unity and love, honoring this profound truth.

Teach me to embrace the diversity of the Body of Christ and to work toward fostering fellowship, reconciliation, and shared purpose among believers. May my life reflect the grace and unity that glorify Your name.

In Jesus's Name,

Amen.

68. You Have a Guaranteed Formula for Joy

Scripture

Philippians 4:4 "Rejoice in the Lord always. I will say it again: Rejoice!." (NIV)

1 Thessalonians 5:18 "Give thanks in all circumstances; for this is God's will for you in Christ Jesus." (NIV)

Highlights

- **Transformational Truth:** At the moment of salvation, you are given the formula for a joyful life by cultivating praise, thanksgiving, and gratitude to God, regardless of circumstances. This formula for joy is directly proportional to the amount of praise and thanksgiving you offer to God.

- **Foundational Word:** "Rejoice" (Greek: *chairō*) means to be glad or delight, and "Give thanks" (Greek: *eucharisteō*) means to express gratitude.

- **Theological Insight:** John Piper states, "Joy in the Lord is both a gift and a command, arising from faith in God's goodness and His promises, even amidst trials."[69]

Grace Power-Up: God Gives You a Formula for Joy

QUESTION 1: EXAMINING GOD'S CHARACTER

How much Joy would be sucked out of your life if you stopped praising and thanking the Lord God?

---

[69] John Piper, *Desiring God: Meditations of a Christian Hedonist* (Colorado Springs, CO: Multnomah, 2003), p. 33.

QUESTION 2: CURRENT CIRCUMSTANCES

What if today you adopted an attitude of "Praising the Lord No Matter what!" Would you be able to find peace and contentment, even in trials or challenges?

QUESTION 3: FUTURE PLANS - KNOWING THIS TRUTH

How can you intentionally cultivate joy and gratitude in your daily life, reflecting God's goodness to those around you?

A Prayer of Gratitude for the Formula for Joy

Heavenly Father,

Thank You for giving me the formula for joy in every circumstance through praise, thanksgiving, and trust in Your sovereign will. I am grateful for the gift of joy that comes from knowing and relying on You.

Help me to live a life of gratitude, finding peace and contentment in Your goodness and promises, even in difficult times. May my joy and thankfulness reflect Your glory and inspire others to seek the same in You.

In Jesus's Name,

Amen

Formula for a joyful life:

PRAISE + THANKSGIVING (to GOD) = JOY

69. You Are a Member of the Church (Jews and Gentiles Together)

Scripture

Ephesians 3:8-9 "Although I am less than the least of all the Lord's people, this grace was given me: to preach to the Gentiles the boundless riches of Christ, and to make plain to everyone the administration of this mystery, which for ages past was kept hidden in God, who created all things." (NIV)

Colossians 1:18 "And he is the head of the body, the church; he is the beginning and the firstborn from among the dead, so that in everything he might have the supremacy." (NIV)

Highlights

- **Transformational Truth:** At the moment of salvation, you are incorporated into the Church, the Body of Christ, united in purpose to proclaim God's plan of salvation to the world.

- **Foundational Word:** "Church" (Greek: *ekklesia*) refers to the called-out assembly of believers, and "Body of Christ" emphasizes the collective unity of all members under Christ's leadership.

- **Theological Insight:** Dr. Sam Vinton, Jr. writes, "The Church, as the Body of Christ, is not a human institution but a divine mystery revealed through the Apostle Paul. It exists to demonstrate God's manifold wisdom to the world and beyond."[70]

Grace Power-Up: Made a Member of the Church

QUESTION 1: EXAMINING GOD'S CHARACTER

How would your understanding of God's wisdom and grace be limited if He had **not** revealed the mystery of the Church, uniting believers as the Body of Christ?

---

[70] Sam Vinton, Jr., *The Church: God's Masterpiece of Grace* (Grand Rapids, MI: Grace Publications, 2005), p. 72.

QUESTION 2: CURRENT CIRCUMSTANCES

How does knowing you are a vital member of the Church, the Body of Christ, inspire you to actively participate in proclaiming God's plan of salvation?

QUESTION 3: FUTURE PLANS - KNOWING THIS TRUTH

How can you contribute to the Body of Christ through your actions and witness?

A Prayer of Gratitude for Being Made a Member of the Church

Heavenly Father, thank You for revealing the mystery of the Church and making me a member of the Body of Christ. I am grateful for the grace that unites all believers under Your purpose and leadership. Help me to live as an active and faithful member of Your Church, reflecting Your wisdom and love.

Teach me to proclaim Your salvation boldly and to demonstrate Your manifold wisdom through my words and actions. May my life glorify You and further the mission of the Church to reach others with the Gospel of Christ and train them to serve Him.

In Jesus's Name, Amen.

70. You Are Given the Body of Christ as an Example for Marriage

Scripture

Ephesians 5:28-32 "In this same way, husbands ought to love their wives as their own bodies. He who loves his wife loves himself. After all, no one ever hated their own body, but they feed and care for their body, just as Christ does the church—for we are members of his body. For this reason a man will leave his father and mother and be united to his wife, and the two will become one flesh." This is a profound mystery, but I am talking about Christ and the church." (NIV)

Highlights

- **Transformational Truth:** At the moment of salvation, divine mysteries that were previously hidden are revealed, such as the spiritual parallel between the relationship of Christ and the Church and the union of husband and wife.

- **Foundational Word:** "Marriage" (Greek: *gamos*) signifies a union or covenant, often emphasizing the joining together of two individuals into a sacred relationship. Biblically, it represents the "*agapē*" love by God, reflecting the intimate and eternal relationship between Christ and His Church.

- **Theological Insight:** John MacArthur writes, "The mystery of marriage is that it reflects the greater reality of Christ's love and union with His Church, showing its divine origin and purpose."[71]

---

[71] John MacArthur, *The MacArthur New Testament Commentary: Ephesians* (Chicago, IL: Moody Publishers, 1986), p. 304.

Grace Power-Up: The Parallel of the Mystery of Marriage Revealed

QUESTION 1: EXAMINING GOD'S CHARACTER

How would your understanding of love and marriage be impacted if God had **not** revealed the profound mystery of Christ's relationship with the Church through marriage?

_____

_____

QUESTION 2: CURRENT CIRCUMSTANCES

How does seeing marriage as a reflection of Christ's love for the Church inspire you to approach relationships with greater love, selflessness, and commitment?

_____

_____

QUESTION 3: FUTURE PLANS - KNOWING THIS TRUTH

How can you live out the truth of this mystery, in your marriage or by supporting and honoring the sanctity of marriage as a testimony to Christ's love?

_____

_____

A Prayer of Gratitude for Revealing the Mystery of Marriage

Heavenly Father,

Thank You for revealing the profound mystery of marriage as a reflection of Christ's relationship with the Church. I am in awe of the love, unity, and sacrifice that this divine truth embodies. Help me to honor and reflect this mystery in my life and relationships. Teach me to approach marriage with selflessness and commitment, inspired by Christ's sacrificial love for His Church. May my life and relationships glorify You and point others to the beauty of Christ's love of for His Body, the church. In Jesus's Name, Amen.

The Believer's Strength in Christ

71. You Can Approach God with Freedom and Confidence

Scripture

Ephesians 3:11-12 "According to his eternal purpose that he accomplished in Christ Jesus our Lord. In him and through faith in him we may approach God with freedom and confidence." (NIV)

Hebrews 4:16 "Let us then approach God's throne of grace with confidence, so that we may receive mercy and find grace to help us in our time of need." (NIV)

Highlights

- **Transformational Truth:** At the moment of salvation, you are given the privilege to approach God with boldness and confidence, assured of your acceptance through faith in Christ.

- **Foundational Word:** "Boldness" (Greek: *parrēsia*) signifies fearless openness, and "Access" (Greek: *prosagōgē*) denotes a direct introduction or approach.

- **Theological Insight:** John Stott explains, "Through Christ, believers are no longer distant from God but enjoy unrestricted access to Him with confidence."[72]

Grace Power-Up: Approach God with Freedom and Confidence

QUESTION 1: EXAMINING GOD'S CHARACTER

How would your relationship with God be affected if you couldn't approach Him with boldness and confidence, leaving you distant and uncertain of His acceptance?

---

[72] John Stott, *The Message of Ephesians: God's New Society* (Downers Grove, IL: InterVarsity Press, 1979), p. 104.

_____

_____

_____

QUESTION 2: CURRENT CIRCUMSTANCES

How does knowing you can freely and confidently approach God encourage you to bring your struggles, needs, and praises to Him without hesitation?

_____

_____

_____

QUESTION 3: FUTURE PLANS - KNOWING THIS TRUTH

How can you grow in your relationship with God by regularly approaching Him with freedom and confidence through prayer and faith?

_____

_____

_____

A Prayer of Gratitude for Freedom and Confidence to Approach God

Heavenly Father,

Thank You for giving me the privilege to approach You with freedom and confidence through Christ. I am humbled and grateful that I can come into Your presence without fear, knowing that I am accepted and loved. Help me to trust in this truth and rely on it daily.

Teach me to bring my struggles, needs, and praises to You openly and boldly, growing deeper in my relationship with You. May my life reflect the joy and peace of being fully accepted in Your presence.

In Jesus's Name,
Amen.

72. You Can Now Stand Firm in Christ

Scripture

2 Corinthians 1:21 "Now it is God who makes both us and you stand firm in Christ. He anointed us." (NIV)

Highlights

- **Transformational Truth:** At the moment of salvation, God gives you the ability to stand firm in Christ. This firm foundation is not based on your own strength but on the power, stability, and assurance that come from being established in Him.
- **Foundational Word:** "Stand" (Greek: histēmi) means to be set in place, firmly established, or unwavering. It reflects God's action of positioning believers securely in Christ, enabling them to endure and remain faithful.
- **Theological Insight:** Charles Baker observes, "To stand firm in Christ is to be securely rooted in the grace and truth of the Gospel. It is God who establishes us, making our position in Christ unshakable and eternal."[73]

Grace Power-Up: Standing Firm in Christ

QUESTION 1: EXAMINING GOD'S CHARACTER

When you ask a fellow believer how they are doing and they respond, "Hanging in there," you can confidently reply, "Jesus Christ already did the hanging; you, my brother, are standing firm!" What does this say about God's character?

---

[73] Baker, Charles F., *Understanding God's Purpose*. Grace Publications, Grand Rapids, MI (1994). p. 89.

QUESTION 2: CURRENT CIRCUMSTANCES

What challenges are you facing that require you to stand firm in Christ? How can you lean on His power and promises in these moments?

_____

_____

_____

QUESTION 3: FUTURE PLANS - KNOWING THIS TRUTH

How can you encourage others to stand firm in their faith, trusting in God's ability to establish and sustain them?

_____

_____

_____

A Prayer of Gratitude for Standing Firm in Christ

Heavenly Father, thank You for establishing me in Christ and giving me the strength to stand firm. I am grateful that my foundation is not dependent on my own efforts but on Your power and faithfulness.

Help me to remain steadfast in faith, trusting in Your promises and grace, especially during times of trial or uncertainty. Teach me to rely on Your Spirit and Your Word for strength and to stand boldly as a witness to Your truth and love.

Thank You for securing my position in Christ and for the assurance of Your unshakable Word.

In Jesus's Name,

Amen.

73. You Experience Diversity and Unity in the Body of Christ

Scripture

1 Corinthians 12:12-13 "Just as a body, though one, has many parts, but all its many parts form one body, so it is with Christ. For we were all baptized by one Spirit so as to form one body—whether Jews or Gentiles, slave or free—and we were all given the one Spirit to drink." (NIV)

Highlights

- **Transformational Truth:** At the moment of salvation, you are united into the Body of Christ, a diverse community of individuals with unique gifts and roles, working together in harmony under Christ.

- **Foundational Word:** "Body" (Greek: *sōma*) refers to the collective unity of believers, with each member fulfilling a distinct role.

- **Theological Insight:** John MacArthur explains, "The Church is a perfect blend of unity and diversity, with every believer's uniqueness contributing to the effective functioning of the whole body."[74]

Grace Power-Up: Unified with the Greatest Diversity in the Body of Christ

QUESTION 1: EXAMINING GOD'S CHARACTER

How would your understanding of God's wisdom and grace change if He had **not** designed the Church to be a unified body enriched by its diversity?

---

[74] John MacArthur, *The MacArthur New Testament Commentary:* 1 Corinthians (Chicago, IL: Moody Publishers, 1984), p. 295.

QUESTION 2: CURRENT CIRCUMSTANCES

How does knowing that every believer, regardless of background or role, is an essential part of the Body of Christ encourage you to value your own contributions and those of others?

QUESTION 3: FUTURE PLANS - KNOWING THIS TRUTH

How can you use your unique gifts to serve and strengthen the Body of Christ, promoting harmony and purpose?

A Prayer of Gratitude for Unity and Diversity in the Body of Christ

Heavenly Father,

Thank You for uniting me into the Body of Christ, a perfect blend of unity and diversity. I am grateful for the unique gifts and roles You have given me and each believer, contributing to the effective functioning of the Church. Help me to value and embrace the diversity within Your body.

Teach me to use my gifts faithfully and to promote harmony and love among believers. May my life and actions reflect the unity and purpose You have designed for the Body of Christ, glorifying Your name.

In Jesus's Name, Amen.

74. You Can Embrace Weakness for God's Glory

Scripture

2 Corinthians 12:9 "But he said to me, 'My grace is sufficient for you, for my power is made perfect in weakness.' Therefore I will boast all the more gladly about my weaknesses, so that Christ's power may rest on me." (NIV)

Highlights

- **Transformational Truth:** At the moment of salvation, your weakness becomes an opportunity for God's strength to be magnified in your life, to display His power and bring glory to Himself.
- **Foundational Word:** "Weakness" (Greek: astheneia) signifies human frailty and limitations, through which God's strength is perfected.
- **Theological Insight:** Don Smith writes, "It glorifies God to unmistakably reveal His power through the weak."[75]

Grace Power-Up: Embracing Weakness for God's Glory

QUESTION 1: EXAMINING GOD'S CHARACTER

Where would you turn for strength and hope if God's power was **not** made perfect in your weakness?

_____

_____

_____

---

[75] Don Smith, *Portraits of Christ: Commentary on Judges 13-16*. Blue Letter Bible.

QUESTION 2: CURRENT CIRCUMSTANCES

How does recognizing your weaknesses as opportunities for God to work bring confidence and courage in your struggles?

___

___

___

QUESTION 3: FUTURE PLANS - KNOWING THIS TRUTH

How can you rely on God's strength in an area of your life where you feel most inadequate or frail?

___

___

___

A Prayer of Gratitude for God's Strength in My Weakness

Heavenly Father, thank You for the gift of Your grace, which is sufficient for every need. I praise You for using my weaknesses to display Your strength and bring glory to Yourself.

Help me to embrace my frailties, knowing that Your power is perfected in them. When I feel inadequate or overwhelmed, remind me to lean on You and not my own strength. Teach me to rest in Your sufficiency and to trust in Your plans.

May my life be a testimony of Your power and grace, drawing others closer to You.

In Jesus's Name,

Amen.

75. You Are Delivered from the Law

Scripture

Romans 6:14 "For sin shall no longer be your master, because you are not under the law, but under grace." (NIV)

Romans 7:6 "But now, by dying to what once bound us, we have been released from the law so that we serve in the new way of the Spirit, and not in the old way of the written code." (NIV)

2 Corinthians 3:11 "And if what was transitory came with glory, how much greater is the glory of that which lasts." (NIV)

Galatians 3:25 "Now that this faith has come, we are no longer under a guardian." (NIV)

Highlights

- **Transformational Truth:** At the moment of salvation, you are delivered from the law's authority and condemnation, set free to live under the grace of God through Christ.
- **Foundational Word:** "Law" (*Greek: nomos*) refers to the divine commandments and regulations that once governed moral and ceremonial behavior, now fulfilled and transcended by Christ's grace.
- **Theological Insight**: Dr. Sam Vinton, Jr. shares "The law pointed us to Christ, but now, being in Him, we are set free from its demands, empowered to live by grace through the Spirit."[76]

Grace Power-Up: Delivered from the Law

QUESTION 1: EXAMINING GOD'S CHARACTER

How would your ability to live freely in God's grace be affected if He had **not** delivered you from the law's authority and condemnation, bound to its impossible demands?

---

[76] Sam Vinton, Jr., *Set Free by Grace: Living in the Power of the Spirit* (Grand Rapids, MI: Grace Publications, 2009), p. 92.

QUESTION 2: CURRENT CIRCUMSTANCES

How does knowing you are no longer under the law but under grace empower you to serve God joyfully through the Spirit instead of striving to meet the law's demands?

QUESTION 3: FUTURE PLANS - KNOWING THIS TRUTH

How can you use your freedom from the law to demonstrate God's grace and reflect His love in your relationships and daily actions?

A Prayer of Gratitude for Deliverance from the Law

Heavenly Father, thank You for delivering me from the law's authority and condemnation, setting me free to live under Your grace through Christ. I am grateful for the new way of the Spirit, which empowers me to serve You joyfully and without fear of failure.

Help me to embrace this freedom with humility and gratitude, using it to reflect Your love and grace to others. Teach me to live in the fullness of Your Spirit, glorifying You through my words, actions, and faith.

In Jesus's Name,

Amen.

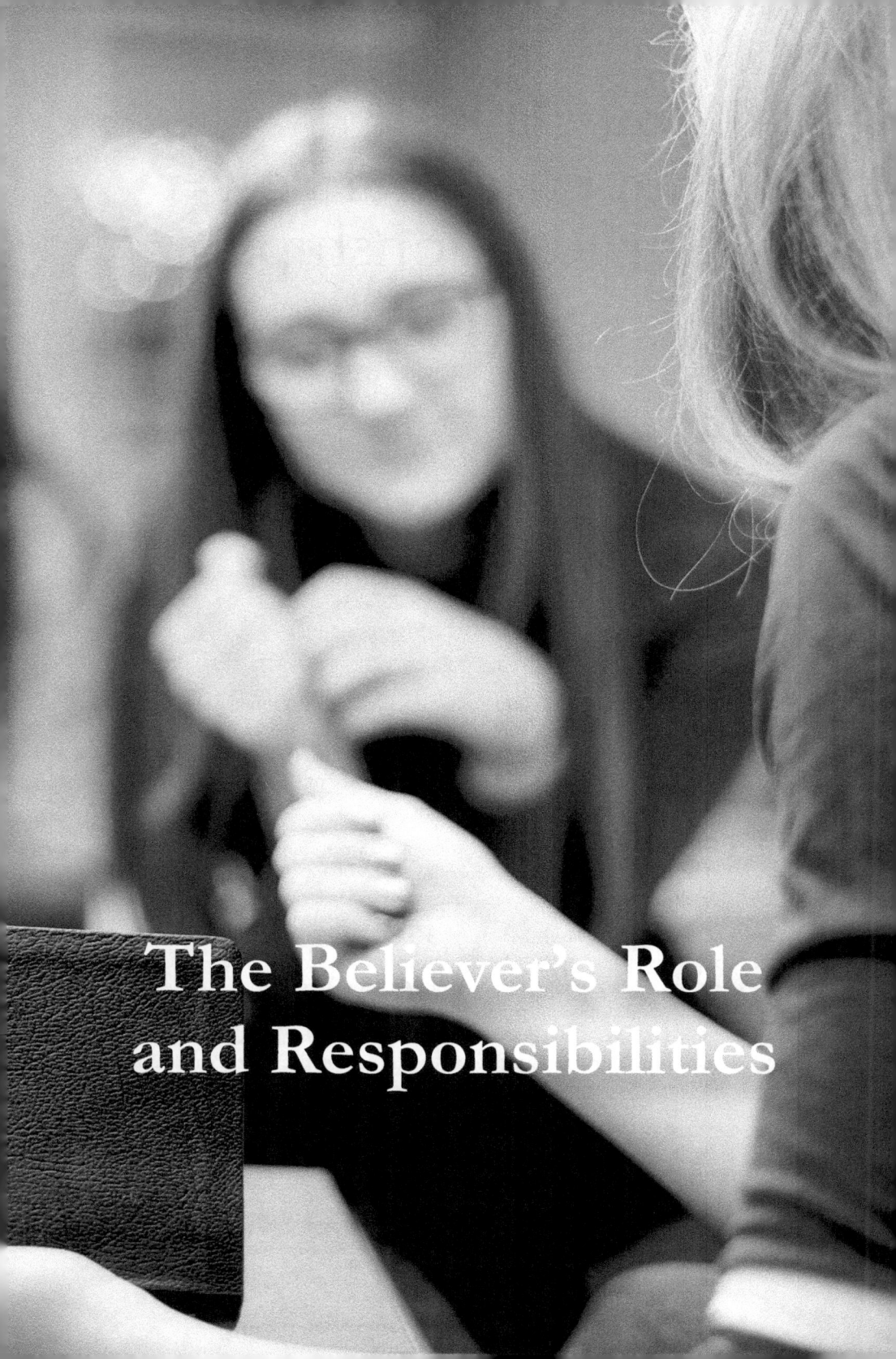

The Believer's Role and Responsibilities

76. You Have Supernatural Power for Relationships

Scripture

2 Corinthians 3:18 "And we all, who with unveiled faces contemplate the Lord's glory, are being transformed into his image with ever-increasing glory." (NIV)

2 Corinthians 5:17 "Therefore, if anyone is in Christ, the new creation has come: The old has gone, the new is here."

Ephesians 4:20–24 "Throw off your old sinful nature and your former way of life, which is corrupted by lust and deception. Instead, let the Spirit renew your thoughts and attitudes." (NIV)

Highlights

- **Transformational Truth:** At the moment of salvation, you are given the supernatural power to develop relationships that can impact others for eternity, reflecting Christ's transformative love and grace. This transformation equips us to love and influence others in ways that mirror God's redemptive work.

- **Foundational Word:** "Transformed" (Greek: *metamorphoō*) means to change into another form, emphasizing an ongoing, inward renewal that results in outward Christlike behavior.

- **Theological Insight:** Ken Kemper shared transformational relationships this way, "Christ's transformative power enables believers to cultivate relationships that mirror His love, serving as instruments of change and demonstrating the eternal significance of being 'in Christ'."[77] John Gowdy: "The grace of God not only changes our destiny but transforms our daily interactions, calling us to reflect Christ's redemptive work in every relationship we encounter."[78]

---

[77] Ken Kemper, *Living in Christ: Reflections on Discipleship and Relationship* (Grand Rapids, MI: Grace Publications, 2018), p. 89.

[78] John Gowdy, *Grace in Action: Living Out Christ's Redemption Daily* (Green Valley, AZ: Redemption Press, 2020), p. 112.

Grace Power-Up: Supernatural Power for Transformational Relationships

QUESTION 1: EXAMINING GOD'S CHARACTER

How would your relationships be affected if God's transformative power were **not** available, leaving you unable to reflect His love and grace in your interactions with others?

\
\
\

QUESTION 2: CURRENT CIRCUMSTANCES

How does knowing you are being transformed into Christ's image encourage you to approach your relationships with greater love, forgiveness, and intentionality?

\
\
\

QUESTION 3: FUTURE PLANS - KNOWING THIS TRUTH

How can you intentionally cultivate relationships that reflect Christ's transformative power, impacting others for eternity through love and grace?

A Prayer of Gratitude for Supernatural Power in Transformational Relationships

Heavenly Father,

Thank You for the supernatural power You provide to transform my relationships, equipping me to reflect Christ's love and grace. I am grateful for the ongoing work of Your Spirit, renewing my heart and mind to build relationships that glorify You and impact others for eternity.

Help me to grow in Christlike love, forgiveness, and intentionality in all my interactions. Teach me to be an instrument of Your redemptive work, drawing others closer to You through the way I live and love, and reliance upon Your Word.

In Jesus's Name,
Amen.

PAUSE AND THINK

What transformational relationships is the Lord prompting you to develop to impact others for His glory?

Write down the names of individuals the Lord puts on your heart:

_____

_____

_____

_____

_____

_____

_____

77. You Win Spiritual Battles on Your Knees

Scripture

Ephesians 6:12 "For our struggle is not against flesh and blood, but against the rulers, against the authorities, against the powers of this dark world and against the spiritual forces of evil in the heavenly realms." (NIV)

Highlights

- **Transformational Truth:** At the moment of salvation, you are given prayer as a powerful tool for overcoming spiritual battles, inviting God's intervention and strength against the forces of darkness.
- **Foundational Word:** "Prayer" (Greek: *proseuchē*) signifies communion with God, serving as both a defensive and offensive weapon in spiritual warfare.
- **Theological Insight:** John Piper writes, "Prayer is the means by which we align ourselves with the purposes of God and draw on His power to overcome opposition."[79]

Grace Power-Up: Overcoming Spiritual Battles on your Knees

QUESTION 1: EXAMINING GOD'S CHARACTER

How would your ability to face spiritual battles be different if God had **not** given you the powerful tool of prayer, leaving you to rely solely on your own strength?

_____

_____

---

[79] John Piper, *Let the Nations Be Glad: The Supremacy of God in Missions* (Grand Rapids, MI: Baker Academic, 2003), p. 65.

QUESTION 2: CURRENT CIRCUMSTANCES

How does knowing you can turn to God through prayer in the midst of spiritual battles provide you with encouragement and confidence to persevere?

QUESTION 3: FUTURE PLANS - KNOWING THIS TRUTH

How does reading the first few chapters of Nehemiah help you cultivate a consistent prayer life and align yourself with God's purposes and draw on His power to overcome spiritual opposition, by winning all your spiritual battles on your knees?

A Prayer of Gratitude for the Gift of Prayer in Spiritual Battles

Heavenly Father,

Thank You for the gift of prayer, which allows me to draw on Your strength and align myself with Your purposes in the face of spiritual battles. I am grateful that I do not have to rely on my own power but can call on You to fight for me.

Help me to cultivate a consistent and fervent prayer life, trusting in Your Word and power to overcome the forces of darkness. May my prayers glorify You and be a testimony to the strength and peace found in communion with You.

In Jesus's Name,
Amen.

78. You Can Trust God's Sovereignty over Revenge

Scripture

Romans 12:19 "Do not take revenge, my dear friends, but leave room for God's wrath, for it is written: 'It is mine to avenge; I will repay,' says the Lord." (NIV)

2 Thessalonians 1:6-8 "God is just: He will pay back trouble to those who trouble you and give relief to you who are troubled, and to us as well. This will happen when the Lord Jesus is revealed from heaven in blazing fire with his powerful angels. He will punish those who do not know God and do not obey the gospel of our Lord Jesus." (NIV)

Highlights

- **Transformational Truth:** At the moment of salvation, you are freed from the need for revenge, payback, or personal justice. You are learning to trust in God's sovereignty and His perfect judgment.
- **Foundational Word:** "Avenge" (Greek: ekdikeō) means to exact justice or retribution, a role that belongs to God alone.
- **Theological Insight**: Charles Baker: "When we trust God's sovereignty, we relinquish the burden of revenge and find peace in knowing that His justice is perfect and His timing unfailing."[80]

Grace Power-Up: Trusting God's Sovereignty over Revenge

QUESTION 1: EXAMINING GOD'S CHARACTER

How would your peace and relationships be affected if you could **not** trust God's perfect justice, leaving you to carry the burden of revenge and personal retribution?

---

[80] Charles Baker, *Understanding God's Sovereignty: Trusting His Justice and Timing* (Grand Rapids, MI: Grace Bible Press, 1965), p. 132.

QUESTION 2: CURRENT CIRCUMSTANCES

How does trusting in God's sovereignty over justice help you release anger and bitterness when you've been wronged?

QUESTION 3: FUTURE PLANS - KNOWING THIS TRUTH

How can you practice trusting God with situations where you feel the need for justice, reflecting faith in His perfect judgment?

A Prayer of Gratitude for Trusting God's Sovereignty over Revenge

Heavenly Father,

Thank You for freeing me from the burden of seeking revenge by teaching me to trust in Your perfect justice and sovereignty. I am grateful that You see every wrong and will bring about justice in Your way and timing.

Help me to let go of anger and bitterness, trusting You to handle what I cannot. Teach me to reflect Your grace and peace in my responses to those who wrong me, demonstrating my faith in Your ultimate judgment.

In Jesus's Name,
Amen.

79. You Are Entrusted with the Message of Reconciliation

Scripture

2 Corinthians 5:18-19 "All this is from God, who reconciled us to himself through Christ and gave us the ministry of reconciliation: that God was reconciling the world to himself in Christ, not counting people's sins against them. And he has committed to us the message of reconciliation." (NIV)

Highlights

- **Transformational Truth:** At the moment of salvation, you are not only reconciled, but you are entrusted with the message of reconciliation, tasked with sharing God's offer of peace and restoration with the world.
- **Foundational Word:** "Reconciliation" (Greek: *katallagē*) means the restoration of a relationship, specifically between humanity and God.
- **Theological Insight:** Charles Spurgeon states, "The ministry of reconciliation is the grand design of the gospel, calling sinners to peace with God through Christ."[81]

Grace Power-Up: Given the Message of Reconciliation

QUESTION 1: EXAMINING GOD'S CHARACTER

What would the world's hope for peace and restoration be without God entrusting you with the message of reconciliation through Christ?

_____

_____

_____

---

[81] Charles Spurgeon, *Metropolitan Tabernacle Pulpit*, Vol. 25, Sermon No. 1497: *The Ministry of Reconciliation* (London: Passmore and Alabaster, 1879), p. 314.

QUESTION 2: CURRENT CIRCUMSTANCES

How does knowing you carry the message of reconciliation motivate you to share God's love and truth with others in your daily interactions?

_____

_____

_____

QUESTION 3: FUTURE PLANS - KNOWING THIS TRUTH

How can you actively participate in God's ministry of reconciliation, sharing His message of peace and restoration with those in your sphere of influence?

_____

_____

_____

A Prayer of Gratitude for the Message of Reconciliation

Heavenly Father,

Thank You for reconciling me to Yourself through Christ and entrusting me with the message of reconciliation. I am humbled by the privilege of sharing Your offer of peace and restoration with the world. Help me to proclaim this truth with love, boldness, and compassion.

Teach me to reflect Your heart and Your Word in my actions, calling others to experience the joy and hope of being reconciled to You. May my life glorify You as I fulfill this ministry with faithfulness and grace.

In Jesus's Name,
Amen.

80. You Are Made Alive to Worship and Serve

Scripture

Romans 12:1–2 "Therefore, I urge you, brothers and sisters, in view of God's mercy, to offer your bodies as a living sacrifice, holy and pleasing to God—this is your true and proper worship. Do not conform to the pattern of this world, but be transformed by the renewing of your mind. Then you will be able to test and approve what God's will is—his good, pleasing and perfect will." (NIV)

Highlights

- **Transformational Truth:** At the moment of salvation, you are made alive to serve and worship God. You become living sacrifices, dedicated to the One who saved you and to serving others, so they may see Christ for who He is and what He accomplished on the Cross.

- **Foundational Word:** "Living sacrifice" (Greek: *thysia zōsa*) refers to an ongoing, active offering of oneself to God, reflecting a life dedicated to His glory and service.

- **Theological Insight:** C.R. Stam shares, "True worship is seen in the believer's life of service, where God's grace inspires us to live sacrificially, pointing others to the finished work of Christ on the Cross."[82]

Grace Power-Up: Made Alive to Serve and Worship

QUESTION 1: EXAMINING GOD'S CHARACTER

How would your ability to serve and worship be limited if God had **not** made you spiritually alive, leaving you disconnected from His purpose and unable to glorify Him?

---

[82] C.R. Stam, *True Spiritual Worship: Living a Life of Grace* (Grand Rapids, MI: Berean Bible Society, 1959), p. 142.

QUESTION 2: CURRENT CIRCUMSTANCES

How does knowing that your life is a "living sacrifice" encourage you to serve and worship God wholeheartedly in your daily actions?

QUESTION 3: FUTURE PLANS - KNOWING THIS TRUTH

How can you live out sacrificial service and worship in practical ways, pointing others to the love and grace of Christ?

A Prayer of Gratitude for Being Made Alive to Serve and Worship

Heavenly Father, thank You for making me alive through salvation and giving me the privilege to serve and worship You. I am grateful for the grace that inspires me to live as a living sacrifice, dedicating my life to serving and praising You.

Help me to reflect Your love through sacrificial service, pointing others to the work of Christ on the Cross. Teach me to worship You with my whole heart and to live in a way that pleases You, fulfilling Your good and perfect will.

In Jesus's Name,

Amen.

Living a Transformed Life

81. You Have Freedom through Prayer

Scripture

1 Thessalonians 5:17 "Pray without ceasing." (NIV)

Philippians 4:6-7 "Do not be anxious about anything, but in every situation, by prayer and petition, with thanksgiving, present your requests to God. And the peace of God, which transcends all understanding, will guard your hearts and your minds in Christ Jesus." (NIV)

Highlights

- **Transformational Truth:** At the moment of salvation, you receive the gift of prayer to seek God's strength and intervention to find freedom from depression, discouragement, and self-doubt, leaving all your burdens with Him.
- **Foundational Word:** "Pray without ceasing" (Greek: *adialeiptos proseuchomai*) emphasizes continuous, unwavering prayer as a means of spiritual resilience.
- **Theological Insight**: John MacArthur writes, "Prayer is the believer's lifeline to God, providing peace and strength to persevere through trials and emotional struggles."[83]

Grace Power-Up: Freedom through Prayer

QUESTION 1: EXAMINING GOD'S CHARACTER

How would your ability to face emotional struggles be impacted if God had **not** given you the gift of persistent prayer, leaving you without an opportunity to leave your burdens at the cross and be given His peace and strength?

---

[83] John MacArthur, *Alone with God: Rediscovering the Power and Passion of Prayer* (Colorado Springs, CO: David C. Cook, 1995), p. 42.

QUESTION 2: CURRENT CIRCUMSTANCES

How does engaging in persistent prayer help you navigate feelings of depression or discouragement, reminding you of God's presence and promises?

QUESTION 3: FUTURE PLANS - KNOWING THIS TRUTH

How can you incorporate persistent prayer into your daily routine, fostering resilience and drawing closer to God in every situation?

A Prayer of Gratitude for Freedom through Persistent Prayer

Heavenly Father,

Thank You for the gift of persistent prayer and your desire to take all our burdens which provides peace, strength, and freedom from depression and discouragement. I am grateful that I can turn to You in every situation, knowing You hear my prayers and guard my heart with Your peace.

Help me to cultivate a habit of praying without ceasing, trusting You to sustain me through trials and emotional struggles. May my prayer life reflect my faith in Your goodness and draw others to the hope and peace found in You.

In Jesus's Name,
Amen.

82. You Are Called to a Heavenly Mindset

Scripture

Colossians 3:1-2 "Since, then, you have been raised with Christ, set your hearts on things above, where Christ is, seated at the right hand of God. Set your minds on things above, not on earthly things." (NIV)

Highlights

- **Transformational Truth:** At the moment of salvation, you are raised with Christ and given a heavenly mindset, empowered to live with an eternal perspective which reflects Christ's character.
- **Foundational Word:** "Set your minds" (Greek: *phroneō*) means to focus one's attention and affections on heavenly realities.
- **Theological Insight**: Pastor John Gowdy puts it in perspective, "To set our minds on things above is to embrace God's eternal perspective, reflecting Christ's character in every aspect of life and striving for what matters most to Him."[84]

Grace Power-Up: Called to a Heavenly Mindset

QUESTION 1: EXAMINING GOD'S CHARACTER

How would your ability to focus on what truly matters be different if God had **not** given you the ability to set your mind on heavenly realities, leaving you consumed by earthly distractions?

_____

_____

_____

---

[84] John Gowdy, *Eternal Perspective: Living for What Matters Most* (Green Valley, AZ: Redemption Press, 2022), p. 89.

QUESTION 2: CURRENT CIRCUMSTANCES

How does adopting a heavenly mindset help you navigate daily challenges and prioritize what aligns with God's eternal purposes?

_____

_____

_____

QUESTION 3: FUTURE PLANS - KNOWING THIS TRUTH

How can you intentionally cultivate a mindset focused on things above, allowing Christ's character to shape your decisions, words, and actions?

_____

_____

_____

A Prayer of Gratitude for a Heavenly Mindset

Heavenly Father,

Thank You for giving me the ability to set my mind on heavenly things, focusing on what is eternal and aligning my thoughts with Your purposes. I am grateful for Your Word that allows me to see beyond earthly distractions and to reflect Christ's character in my life.

Help me to keep my heart and mind fixed on You, shaping my decisions and actions according to Your will. May my life glorify You and draw others to the eternal hope found in Christ.

In Jesus's Name,
Amen.

83. You Can Depend on God Completely

Scripture

2 Corinthians 3:5 "Not that we are sufficient in ourselves to claim anything as coming from us, but our sufficiency is from God." (NIV)

Highlights

- **Transformational Truth:** At the moment of salvation, your sufficiency is no longer in yourself but in God.

- **Foundational Word:** "Sufficiency" (Greek: *hikanotēs*) signifies adequacy or competence, derived not from oneself but from God.

- **Theological Insight:** Pastor Harry Bultema lays it out this way, "Our sufficiency rests entirely on God's provision. Human effort, no matter how noble, can never fulfill God's purposes without His grace and strength working through us."[85]

Grace Power-Up: Our Dependence on God

QUESTION 1: EXAMINING GOD'S CHARACTER

How would your confidence and purpose be impacted if God did **not** provide His sufficiency, leaving you to rely solely on your own limited abilities and strength?

_____

_____

_____

---

[85] Harry Bultema, *Living by Grace: God's Provision for Every Need* (Grand Rapids, MI: Kregel Publications, 1954), p. 112.

QUESTION 2: CURRENT CIRCUMSTANCES

How does recognizing your complete dependence on God for wisdom and strength bring peace and humility, especially in times of inadequacy or uncertainty?

_____

_____

_____

QUESTION 3: FUTURE PLANS - KNOWING THIS TRUTH

How can you demonstrate your dependence on God in your daily life, seeking His provision and guidance in all your decisions and actions?

_____

_____

_____

A Prayer of Gratitude for Our Dependence on God

Heavenly Father,

Thank You for teaching me to acknowledge my dependence on You. I am grateful that my sufficiency comes from Your provision and not from my own efforts or abilities. Help me to trust in Your Word and strength in every aspect of my life.

Teach me to approach each day with humility and faith, relying on Your guidance and grace to fulfill Your purposes. May my dependence on You reflect Your glory and point others to Your unfailing love and power.

In Jesus's Name,
Amen.

84. You Are Comforted by the God of All Comfort

Scripture

2 Corinthians 1:3-4 "Praise be to the God and Father of our Lord Jesus Christ, the Father of compassion and the God of all comfort, who comforts us in all our troubles, so that we can comfort those in any trouble with the comfort we ourselves receive from God." (NIV)

Highlights

- **Transformational Truth:** At the moment of salvation, God of all comfort becomes our source of comfort and peace. He meets you in your pain and strengthens you, equipping you to offer the same comfort to others in need.
- **Foundational Word:** "Comfort" (Greek: *paraklesis*) refers to encouragement, consolation, or solace, often given by one who comes alongside to provide help and hope during times of trouble.
- **Theological Insight:** Charles H. Spurgeon writes, "No matter what we may be passing through, God's comfort is ours in abundance, and as He comforts us, He equips us to be His instruments of comfort to others."

Grace Power-Up: Comforted by the God of All Comfort

QUESTION 1: EXAMINING GOD'S CHARACTER

Does All, All, Any in 2 Corinthians 1:3-4, include you? Are you sure? Does it really mean that God can comfort us in all our troubles, so that we can comfort those in any troubles?

_____

_____

QUESTION 2: CURRENT CIRCUMSTANCES

How can experiencing God's comfort in all our circumstances, help you face your challenges?

_____

_____

_____

QUESTION 3: FUTURE PLANS - KNOWING THIS TRUTH

What steps can you take to gently extend God's comfort to someone who is struggling?

_____

_____

_____

A Prayer of Gratitude for God's Comfort

Heavenly Father,

Thank You for being the God of all comfort, who meets me in spite of my sin and fills me with Your peace. I am deeply grateful for the way You strengthen and sustain me through Your Spirit, reminding me that I am never alone.

Help me to trust in Your unfailing love, even in the midst of my pain, and to lean on Your promises for comfort. Teach me to extend the same comfort I have received from You to others who are hurting, becoming a vessel of Your compassion and grace.

Thank You for being my refuge and my ever-present help in times of need.

In Jesus's Name,
Amen.

85. You Are Free to Forgive

Scripture

Colossians 3:13 "Bear with each other and forgive one another if any of you has a grievance against someone. Forgive as the Lord forgave you." (NIV)

Highlights

- **Transformational Truth:** At the moment of salvation, Christ's gift of forgiveness becomes your example of showing forgiveness to others. Forgiveness is a gift the Good Lord gives to us, which we can then pass on to others, regardless of their response. This gift fosters healing, restoration, and freedom in relationships.
- **Foundational Word:** "Forgive" (Greek: *charizomai*) means to grant grace or pardon, releasing others from guilt or offense.
- **Theological Insight:** Ken Kemper states, "Forgiveness reflects the heart of Christ, enabling us to restore relationships by extending the same grace we have received from Him."[86]

Grace Power-Up: Free to Forgive

QUESTION 1: EXAMINING GOD'S CHARACTER

How would your ability to forgive and heal relationships be impacted if God had **not** first forgiven you, leaving you bound by bitterness and unresolved offenses?

_____

_____

_____

---

[86] Ken Kemper, *Living Grace: Extending Forgiveness and Reflecting Christ* (Grand Rapids, MI: Grace Publications, 2020), p. 112.

QUESTION 2: CURRENT CIRCUMSTANCES

How does knowing you are forgiven by Christ enable you to extend grace and forgiveness to others, especially when it feels undeserved?

_____

_____

_____

QUESTION 3: FUTURE PLANS - KNOWING THIS TRUTH

How can you practice forgiveness in your relationships, reflecting Christ's grace and fostering healing and freedom?

_____

_____

_____

A Prayer of Gratitude for the Freedom to Forgive

Heavenly Father,

Thank You for the gift of forgiveness, which You have freely given through Christ. I am grateful for the freedom it brings, allowing me to extend grace and restore relationships. Help me to forgive others as You have forgiven me, reflecting Your love and mercy.

Teach me to let go of bitterness and to embrace forgiveness as a way to heal and build stronger, Christ-centered relationships. May my life be a testimony of Your grace, pointing others to the power of forgiveness in You.

In Jesus's Name,
Amen.

Eternity and Assurance

86. You Can Cultivate an Un-offendable Heart

Scripture

Colossians 3:12–14 "Therefore, as God's chosen people, holy and dearly loved, clothe yourselves with compassion, kindness, humility, gentleness and patience. Bear with each other and forgive one another if any of you has a grievance against someone. Forgive as the Lord forgave you. And over all these virtues put on love, which binds them all together in perfect unity." (NIV)

Ephesians 4:2 "Be completely humble and gentle; be patient, bearing with one another in love." (NIV)

Highlights

- **Transformational Truth:** At the moment of salvation, you are given the ability to develop an un-offendable heart, rising above the natural inclination to take offense and embracing forgiveness, humility, love, grace, and wisdom. This transformation reflects God's truth and is empowered by His Spirit.
- **Foundational Word:** "Forgiveness" (Greek: aphesis) means to release or let go, freeing both the giver and the recipient from the burden of offense.
- **Theological Insight:** Pastor John Gowdy shares, "An un-offendable heart is the mark of a life transformed by Christ, choosing grace over grievance and embodying His love in every interaction."[87]

Grace Power-Up: Cultivating an Un-offendable Heart

---

[87] John Gowdy, *Grace in Action: Living with an Un-offendable Heart* (Green Valley, AZ: Redemption Press, 2022), p. 78.

QUESTION 1: EXAMINING GOD'S CHARACTER

How would your relationships and peace be affected if God had **not** modeled forgiveness and grace, leaving you without the example or strength to let go of offenses?

_____

_____

QUESTION 2: CURRENT CIRCUMSTANCES

How does embracing an un-offendable heart, rooted in Christ's love and forgiveness, help you navigate conflict and maintain unity in your relationships?

_____

_____

QUESTION 3: FUTURE PLANS - KNOWING THIS TRUTH

How can you actively cultivate an un-offendable heart, giving forgiveness as a gift over offense in your daily interactions?

_____

_____

A Prayer of Gratitude for the Gift of an Un-offendable Heart

Heavenly Father,

Thank You for empowering me through Your Spirit to cultivate an un-offendable heart. I am grateful for Your example of grace and forgiveness, which teaches me to rise above offenses and choose love instead.

Help me to embody Christ's character in my interactions, letting go of grievances and reflecting compassion, humility, and patience. May my life be a testimony of Your transforming power and inspire others to embrace forgiveness and grace.

In Jesus's Name,
Amen.

87. You Are Equipped with the Power of God's Word

Scripture

Ephesians 6:17 "Take the helmet of salvation and the sword of the Spirit, which is the word of God." (NIV)

Hebrews 4:12 "For the word of God is alive and active. Sharper than any double-edged sword, it penetrates even to dividing soul and spirit, joints and marrow; it judges the thoughts and attitudes of the heart." (NIV)

Highlights

- **Transformational Truth:** At the moment of salvation, you are given the Word of God as a powerful tool to defend against and fight off any advances from evil forces in the world. The Word equips you for spiritual battle and strengthens you to stand firm in truth.

- **Foundational Word:** "Word" (Greek: Logos) Refers to the eternal, universal, and living Word of God, embodying divine wisdom and truth. It represents Christ Himself as the Word made flesh (John 1:1) and the full revelation of God. "Word" (Greek: Rhema) Refers to the spoken, active, and specific Word of God, often applied in particular situations to defeat spiritual opposition and bring clarity or revelation.

- **Theological Insight:** Dr. Ken Kemper's powerful words, "The Word of God is both a shield and a sword, providing protection and power for the believer to navigate life's spiritual challenges with confidence in God's truth."[88]

Grace Power-Up: Power Tool: The Word of God

---

[88] Ken Kemper, *Equipped by the Word: Living with Power and Protection* (Grand Rapids, MI: Grace Publications, 2020), p. 115.

QUESTION 1: EXAMINING GOD'S CHARACTER

How would your spiritual battles be affected if God had **not** provided His Word as a tool for defense and truth, leaving you unarmed against evil forces?

_____

_____

QUESTION 2: CURRENT CIRCUMSTANCES

How does relying on the Word of God equip you to stand firm in truth and resist spiritual opposition in your daily life?

_____

_____

QUESTION 3: FUTURE PLANS - KNOWING THIS TRUTH

How can you actively use God's Word as both a shield and a sword to guide your decisions, strengthen your faith, and share His truth with others?

_____

_____

_____

A Prayer of Gratitude for the Word of God

Heavenly Father,

Thank You for giving me Your Word as a powerful tool to defend against evil and stand firm in truth. I am grateful for its living and active power, which equips me for spiritual battles and strengthens my faith.

Help me to immerse myself in Your Word daily, using it to guide my thoughts, decisions, and actions. Teach me to wield it effectively as both a shield and a sword, glorifying You and sharing Your truth with confidence and love.

In Jesus's Name, Amen.

88. You Are Dead to the Law

Scripture

Romans 7:4 "So, my brothers and sisters, you also died to the law through the Body of Christ, that you might belong to another, to him who was raised from the dead, in order that we might bear fruit for God." (NIV)

Highlights

- **Transformational Truth:** At the moment of salvation, you are freed from the authority of the law through your union with Christ's death and resurrection, enabling you to live under grace.
- **Foundational Word:** "Dead" (*Greek: thanatoō*) means to be put to death or rendered inactive, symbolizing the believer's separation from the law's power.
- **Theological Insight:** Martin Luther states, "Through Christ, the law is satisfied, and we are freed from its condemning power, called to live in the righteousness of faith."[89]

Grace Power-Up: Dead to the Law

QUESTION 1: EXAMINING GOD'S CHARACTER

How would your relationship with God be impacted if He had **not** freed you from the law's condemning power, leaving you bound to its demands and unable to live under grace?

_____

_____

_____

---

[89] Martin Luther, *Commentary on Galatians* (1535), translated by Erasmus Middleton, p. 85.

QUESTION 2: CURRENT CIRCUMSTANCES

How does knowing you are no longer bound by the law but alive in Christ empower you to live a life that bears fruit for God?

_____

_____

_____

QUESTION 3: FUTURE PLANS - KNOWING THIS TRUTH

How can you embrace the freedom of living under grace, allowing it to shape your relationships, decisions, and spiritual growth?

_____

_____

_____

A Prayer of Gratitude for Being Dead to the Law

Heavenly Father,

Thank You for freeing me from the authority of the law through Christ's death and for allowing me to live under grace. I am grateful that I no longer stand condemned but belong to Christ, who enables me to bear fruit for Your glory.

Help me to fully embrace this freedom, living a life that reflects Your grace and produces fruit. Teach me to honor You in every aspect of my life, using my freedom to serve and glorify You.

In Jesus's Name,
Amen.

89. You Have Christ as Your Foundation

Scripture

Ephesians 2:19-20 "Consequently, you are no longer foreigners and strangers, but fellow citizens with God's people and also members of his household, built on the foundation of the apostles and prophets, with Christ Jesus himself as the chief cornerstone." (NIV)

1 Corinthians 3:11 "For no one can lay any foundation other than the one already laid, which is Jesus Christ." (NIV)

Highlights

- **Transformational Truth:** At the moment of salvation, Jesus Christ becomes the foundation of your life, providing the stability, strength, and basis for spiritual growth.
- **Foundational Word:** "Foundation" (*Greek: themelios*) refers to the base or cornerstone upon which a structure is built, symbolizing Christ as the essential support and starting point for the believer's faith.
- **Theological Insight:** Charles Swindoll shares, "Christ is the essential foundation for every believer, providing the stability and support we need to grow and stand firm in faith."[90]

Grace Power-Up: Christ as Our Foundation

QUESTION 1: EXAMINING GOD'S CHARACTER

How would your faith and spiritual growth be impacted if Christ were **not** the foundation of your life, leaving you to rely on your own ("sandy" - not firm) foundation?

---

[90] Charles R. Swindoll, *Strengthening Your Grip: How to Be Grounded in a Chaotic World* (Nashville, TN: Thomas Nelson, 2011), p. 48.

QUESTION 2: CURRENT CIRCUMSTANCES

How does knowing that Christ is your foundation provide you with stability and strength during times of uncertainty or spiritual challenges?

QUESTION 3: FUTURE PLANS - KNOWING THIS TRUTH

How can you continue to build your life upon Christ as your foundation, ensuring that every aspect of your faith and actions reflects His stability and truth of God's Word?

A Prayer of Gratitude for Christ as Our Foundation

Heavenly Father, thank You for making Jesus Christ the foundation of my life, providing the stability and strength I need to stand firm in faith and grow spiritually. I am grateful that my life is built on His truth and love, giving me a secure and unshakable base.

Help me to deepen my faith in Christ as my foundation, trusting Him to guide and sustain me in every circumstance. Teach me to build every aspect of my life upon Christ and the Word, reflecting His character and glorifying You.

In Jesus's Name, Amen.

90. You Are God's Temple

Scripture

1 Corinthians 3:16 "Don't you know that you yourselves are God's temple and that God's Spirit dwells in your midst?." (NIV)

1 Corinthians 6:19 "Do you not know that your bodies are temples of the Holy Spirit, who is in you, whom you have received from God? You are not your own." (NIV)

1 Corinthians 3:9 "For we are co-workers in God's service; you are God's field, God's building." (NIV)

Highlights

- **Transformational Truth:** At the moment of salvation, you become God's temple, His dwelling place, and a building that reflects His glory to the world.
- **Foundational Word:** "Temple" (*Greek: naos*) refers to the inner sanctuary or dwelling place of God, signifying the believer as a sacred vessel for His presence.
- **Theological Insight:** Charles Spurgeon writes, "The believer is the temple of God, and as such, every thought, word, and deed should reflect the holiness of the One who dwells within."[91]

Grace Power-Up: You are God's Temple

QUESTION 1: EXAMINING GOD'S CHARACTER

How would your understanding of God's closeness and holiness change if He had **not** chosen to dwell within you, leaving you without His presence as a guiding and sanctifying force?

---

[91] Charles Spurgeon, *Metropolitan Tabernacle Pulpit*, Vol. 25, Sermon No. 1463: *The Temple of the Living God* (London: Passmore and Alabaster, 1879), p. 314.

QUESTION 2: CURRENT CIRCUMSTANCES

How does knowing that you are God's temple, a sacred vessel for His presence, influence the way you think, speak, and act daily?

QUESTION 3: FUTURE PLANS - KNOWING THIS TRUTH

How can you live in a way that honors God's presence within you, ensuring that your life reflects His glory and holiness to the world?

A Prayer of Gratitude for Being God's Temple

Heavenly Father,

Thank You for making me Your temple, a dwelling place for Your Spirit. I am humbled and grateful that You have chosen to reside within me, sanctifying and guiding me in all I do.

Help me to live a life worthy of this calling, reflecting Your holiness and glory in every thought, word, and deed. Teach me to honor Your presence within me and to use my life as a testimony of Your love and grace to the world.

In Jesus's Name,

Amen.

91. You Have God's Undeserved Gift of Love

Scripture

Romans 5:5 "And hope does not put us to shame, because God's love has been poured out into our hearts through the Holy Spirit, who has been given to us."

Romans 5:8 "But God demonstrates his own love for us in this: While we were still sinners, Christ died for us." (NIV)

Highlights

- **Transformational Truth:** At the moment of salvation, you are embraced by the undeserved and unconditional love of God. This love, demonstrated through Christ's sacrificial death, is a gift that cannot be earned. God's grace plain and simple lifting us from sin into eternal life.

- **Foundational Word:** "Love" (Greek: *agapē*) signifies selfless, unconditional love that is rooted in God's nature, not dependent on human worthiness.

- **Theological Insight**: Charles Spurgeon states, "The love of God is entirely unmerited, reaching down to sinners in their lowest state and lifting them up to Himself."[92]

Grace Power-Up: The Underserved Gift of God's Love

QUESTION 1: EXAMINING GOD'S CHARACTER

How would your understanding of God's grace and love change if He only extended His love based on merit, leaving sinners without hope?

---

[92] Charles Spurgeon, *Metropolitan Tabernacle Pulpit*, Vol. 7, Sermon No. 402: *The Unmerited Love of God* (London: Passmore and Alabaster, 1861), p. 263.

QUESTION 2: CURRENT CIRCUMSTANCES

How does knowing that God's love is a free and undeserved gift encourage you to trust Him and share that love with others, even when they may not deserve it?

QUESTION 3: FUTURE PLANS - KNOWING THIS TRUTH

How can you live in gratitude for God's undeserved love, reflecting it in your relationships and actions to point others toward Him?

A Prayer of Gratitude for the Gift of God's Love

Heavenly Father, thank You for the undeserved gift of Your love, demonstrated through Christ's sacrificial death for me. I am humbled by the grace You have shown, reaching down to me while I was still a sinner and lifting me into Your eternal life.

Help me to live in the joy and assurance of receiving Your gift and Your actions of Love demonstrated by Jesus's death, burial and resurrection, sharing it with others even when they don't deserve it. May my life reflect the beauty of Your grace and point others to the hope and salvation found only in Christ.

In Jesus's Name,

Amen.

92. You Are Given an Advocate

Scripture

Romans 8:26-27 "In the same way, the Spirit helps us in our weakness. We do not know what we ought to pray for, but the Spirit himself intercedes for us through wordless groans. And he who searches our hearts knows the mind of the Spirit, because the Spirit intercedes for God's people in accordance with the will of God."

Romans 8:34 "Who then is the one who condemns? No one. Christ Jesus who died—more than that, who was raised to life—is at the right hand of God and is also interceding for us." (NIV)

1 John 2:1 "My dear children, I write this to you so that you will not sin. But if anybody does sin, we have an advocate with the Father—Jesus Christ, the Righteous One." (NIV)

Highlights

- **Transformational Truth:** At the moment of salvation, you are given an advocate in Jesus Christ, who intercedes on your behalf before the Father.

- **Foundational Word:** "Advocate" (*Greek: paraklētos*) means one who comes alongside to help, counsel, or intercede, emphasizing Christ's role as our defender and mediator.

- **Theological Insight:** Charles Spurgeon writes, "In the hour of our need, Jesus stands as our advocate, pleading not our merit, but His blood and righteousness."[93]

Grace Power-Up: Given an Advocate

---

[93] Charles Spurgeon, *Morning and Evening* (London: Passmore and Alabaster, 1866), devotional entry on 1 John 2:1.

QUESTION 1: EXAMINING GOD'S CHARACTER

How would your relationship with God be affected if Christ did **not** serve as your advocate, leaving you to stand alone before the Father?

___

___

___

QUESTION 2: CURRENT CIRCUMSTANCES

How does knowing that Jesus intercedes for you as your advocate give you confidence and peace, especially in moments of failure or weakness?

___

___

___

QUESTION 3: FUTURE PLANS - KNOWING THIS TRUTH

How can you live in gratitude and humility, relying on Christ's advocacy to strengthen your relationship with God and share His grace with others?

___

___

A Prayer of Gratitude for Jesus as Our Advocate

Heavenly Father,

Thank You for giving me Jesus Christ as my advocate, who intercedes on my behalf before You. I am grateful for His perfect righteousness that covers my sin and allows me to approach You with confidence.

Help me to rest in the assurance of His advocacy, trusting in His work and not my own merit. Teach me to reflect this grace by showing compassion and love to others, pointing them to the hope and forgiveness found only in Christ.

In Jesus's Name, Amen.

93. You Are a Co-Laborer with Christ

Scripture

1 Corinthians 3:9 "For we are co-workers in God's service; you are God's field, God's building." (NIV)

2 Corinthians 6:1 "As God's co-workers we urge you not to receive God's grace in vain." (NIV)

Highlights

- **Transformational Truth:** At the moment of salvation, you are united as co-laborers with Christ, participating as fellow laborers.
- **Foundational Word:** "Co-Laborers" (*Greek: synergōs*) means fellow workers or partners, emphasizing the believer's active role in cooperation with Christ's mission.
- **Theological Insight:** A.W. Tozer states, "God invites us into His redemptive work, not because He needs us, but because He desires to use us for His glory and our growth."[94]

Grace Power-Up: Co-Laborers with Christ

QUESTION 1: EXAMINING GOD'S CHARACTER

How would your sense of purpose and value change if God had **not** invited you to be His co-laborer, leaving you without a role in His redemptive work?

_____

_____

_____

---

[94] A.W. Tozer, *The Pursuit of God* (Camp Hill, PA: Christian Publications, 1948), p. 121.

QUESTION 2: CURRENT CIRCUMSTANCES

How does knowing you are a co-laborer with Christ inspire you to approach your daily tasks and relationships as member of the Body of Christ?

_____

_____

_____

QUESTION 3: FUTURE PLANS - KNOWING THIS TRUTH

How can you actively participate as co-laborer's with Christ, using your time, talents, and resources to encourage the Body of Christ?

_____

_____

A Prayer of Gratitude for Being a Co-Laborer with Christ

Heavenly Father,

Thank You for inviting me to be a co-laborer with Christ, participating in Your redemptive work. I am honored and grateful that You choose to use me for Your glory and to build up the Body of Christ.

Help me to approach every aspect of my life with a heavenly focus, using the gifts and opportunities You have given me to serve others and point them to You. Teach me to trust in Your guidance and strength as I work alongside Christ for Your eternal purposes.

In Jesus's Name,
Amen.

94. Your Life is a Letter Written from Heaven

Scripture

2 Corinthians 3:3 "You show that you are a letter from Christ, the result of our ministry, written not with ink but with the Spirit of the living God, not on tablets of stone but on tablets of human hearts." (NIV)

Highlights

- **Transformational Truth:** At the moment of salvation, you become a letter written from heaven, inscribed on your heart by the Spirit, to minister God's truth and love to the world.
- **Foundational Word:** "Letter" (*Greek: epistolē*) refers to a written message, symbolizing the believer as a living testimony of God's work. "Minister" (*Greek: diakonos*) means servant or one who serves, emphasizing the believer's role in sharing God's message through their life and actions.
- **Theological Insight**: Dr. Ken Kemper shares, "The believer is a living letter, written by the Spirit, reflecting the grace and truth of Christ to a watching world."[95]

Grace Power-Up: A Letter Written from Heaven

QUESTION 1: EXAMINING GOD'S CHARACTER

How would the world's understanding of God's love and truth be impacted if you were **not** a letter, written by the Spirit to reflect His grace and truth?

---

[95] Ken Kemper, *Living Letters: Reflecting Christ in a Watching World* (Grand Rapids, MI: Grace Publications, 2018), p. 95.

QUESTION 2: CURRENT CIRCUMSTANCES

How does knowing that you are a letter from Christ encourage you to live in a way that clearly communicates God's truth and love to those around you?

_____

_____

_____

QUESTION 3: FUTURE PLANS - KNOWING THIS TRUTH

How can you allow the Spirit to continue writing His message on your heart, ensuring your life remains a faithful testimony of God's work to a watching world?

_____

_____

_____

A Prayer of Gratitude for Being a Letter Written from Heaven

Heavenly Father, thank You for making me a living letter, written by Your Spirit to reflect Your truth and grace. I am humbled and grateful that You have chosen to use my life as a testimony of Your work to a world in need of Your love.

Help me to live in a way that clearly communicates Your truth and love, allowing the Spirit to write Your message on my heart daily. Teach me to be faithful in sharing Your Word and living as an example of Your transforming power.

In Jesus's Name,

Amen.

95. You Are More than a Conqueror

Scripture

Romans 8:37 "No, in all these things we are more than conquerors through him who loved us." (NIV)

1 Corinthians 15:57 "But thanks be to God, who gives us the victory through our Lord Jesus Christ."

Highlights

- **Transformational Truth:** At the moment of salvation, you are declared more than a conqueror, empowered by the victory of Christ to triumph over sin, death, and all opposition.

- **Foundational Word:** "Conqueror" (*Greek: hypernikaō*) means to overwhelmingly conquer or to be completely victorious, emphasizing the believer's assured victory through Christ's power.

- **Theological Insight:** Erwin Lutzer shares, "In Christ, we are more than conquerors, for His victory over sin and death ensures that nothing can separate us from His love and eternal purposes."[96]

Grace Power-Up: More than a Conqueror

QUESTION 1: EXAMINING GOD'S CHARACTER

How would your confidence and peace be affected if God had **not** declared you victorious in Christ, leaving you to face sin and opposition alone and without assurance of triumph?

_____

_____

_____

[96] Erwin W. Lutzer, *The Vanishing Power of Death: Conquering Sin and Claiming Victory in Christ* (Chicago, IL: Moody Publishers, 2004), p. 132.

QUESTION 2: CURRENT CIRCUMSTANCES

How does knowing you are more than a conqueror through Christ empower you to face challenges, opposition, or fear with faith and strength?

_____

_____

_____

QUESTION 3: FUTURE PLANS - KNOWING THIS TRUTH

How can you live as a conqueror in Christ, using your victory to glorify God and inspire others to trust in His power and love?

_____

_____

_____

A Prayer of Gratitude for Being More than a Conqueror

Heavenly Father,

Thank You for declaring me more than a conqueror through Christ. I am grateful for the victory over sin, death, and opposition that You have secured for me through Your love and power.

Help me to live boldly in the confidence of this victory, facing life's challenges with faith and strength. Teach me to use my triumph to glorify You and to encourage others to trust in Your love and promises.

In Jesus's Name,

Amen.

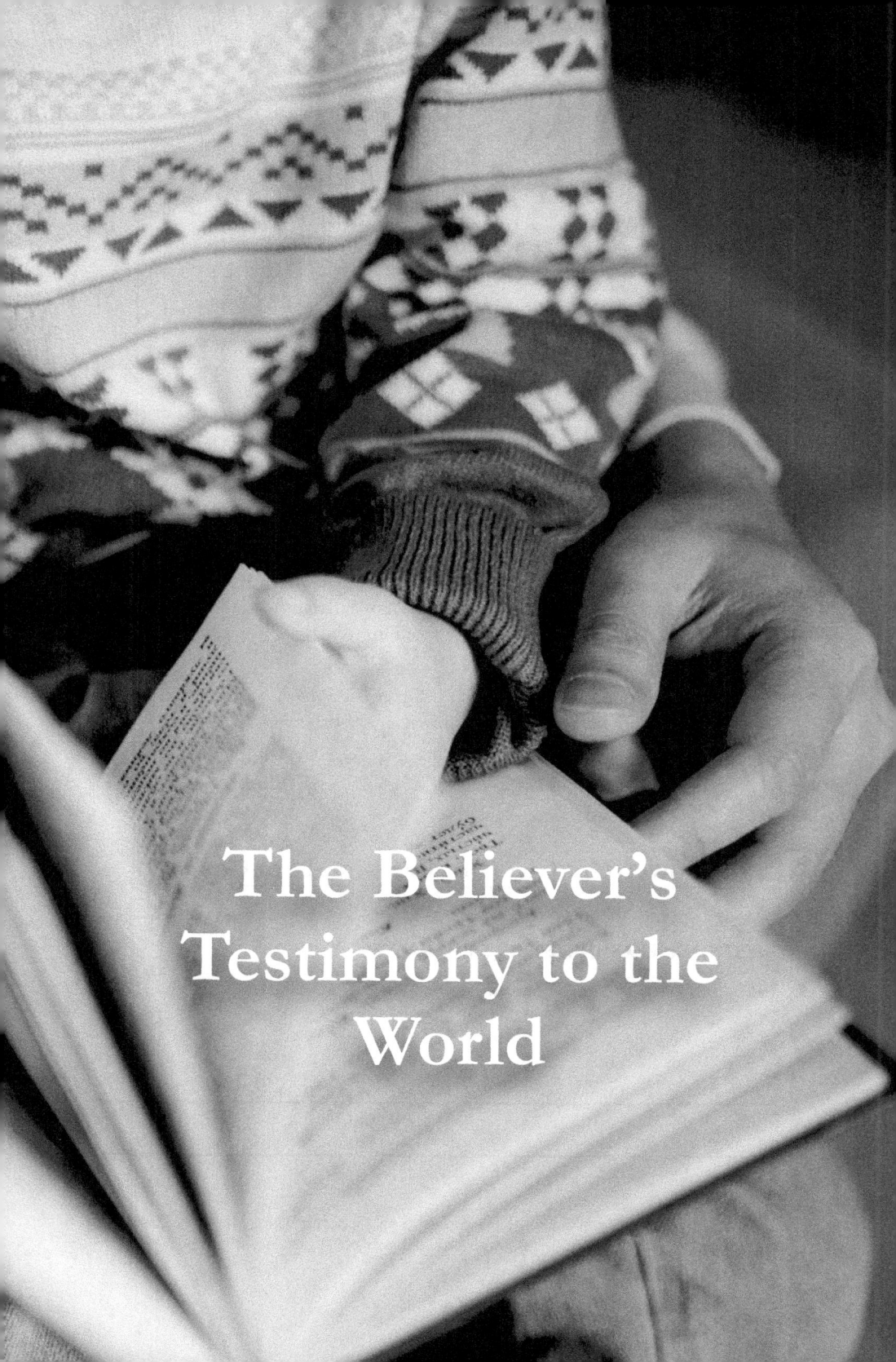

The Believer's Testimony to the World

96. You Are Entrusted with a Simple Gospel to Share

Scripture

1 Corinthians 15:3-4 "For what I received I passed on to you as of first importance: that Christ died for our sins according to the Scriptures, that he was buried, that he was raised on the third day according to the Scriptures." (NIV)

Highlights

- **Transformational Truth:** At the moment of salvation, you are entrusted with the Gospel, a clear and straightforward message of Christ's death, burial, and resurrection, which is the foundation of salvation.
- **Foundational Word:** "Gospel" (Greek: *euangelion*) means good news, emphasizing the simplicity and power of the message.
- **Theological Insight:** Charles Spurgeon notes, "The Gospel is profound in its impact yet simple enough for any believer to proclaim and share with the world."[97]

Grace Power-Up: Given an Easy-to-Share Gospel

QUESTION 1: EXAMINING GOD'S CHARACTER

How would your ability to share the good news be impacted if God had made the Gospel complex and difficult to understand, instead of simple and available for all?

_____

_____

_____

[97] Charles Spurgeon, *Metropolitan Tabernacle Pulpit*, Vol. 25, Sermon No. 1487: *The Simplicity and Power of the Gospel* (London: Passmore and Alabaster, 1879), p. 246.

QUESTION 2: CURRENT CIRCUMSTANCES

How does knowing the Gospel's simplicity and power give you confidence to share it with others, even in situations where you might feel inadequate?

QUESTION 3: FUTURE PLANS - KNOWING THIS TRUTH

How can you intentionally share the clear message of the Gospel with someone in your life this week, trusting in its power to transform?

A Prayer of Gratitude for the Simple and Powerful Gospel

Heavenly Father,

Thank You for entrusting me with the Gospel, a message so simple yet so profound in its power to save. I am grateful for its clarity and for the privilege of sharing it with others. Help me to proclaim it boldly and faithfully, relying on the Holy Spirit to work through my words.

Teach me to trust in the Gospel's power, sharing it with love and confidence, so others may come to know Christ's death, burial, and resurrection and find salvation. May my life reflect the joy and hope of this good news.

In Jesus's Name,
Amen.

97. You Are Given the Gift of Repentance

Scripture

2 Corinthians 7:10 "Godly sorrow brings repentance that leads to salvation and leaves no regret, but worldly sorrow brings death."

2 Timothy 2:25: "Opponents must be gently instructed, in the hope that God will grant them repentance leading them to a knowledge of the truth." (NIV)

Highlights

- **Transformational Truth:** At the moment of salvation, repentance is a gracious gift from God, turning our hearts away from sin and toward Him.
- **Foundational Word:** "Repentance" (*Greek: metanoia*) means a change of mind or turning, signifying a heartfelt decision to turn away from sin and toward God.
- **Theological Insight:** John Calvin: "Repentance and forgiveness are inseparable gifts of grace—repentance being the turning of the heart and forgiveness the free pardon of sins granted by God."[98]

Grace Power-Up: The Gift of Repentance

QUESTION 1: EXAMINING GOD'S CHARACTER

Where would you be if God were unwilling to forgive those who genuinely repent and seek Him?

---

[98] John Calvin, *Institutes of the Christian Religion*, Book III, Chapter 3, Section 20 (Edinburgh: Calvin Translation Society, 1845).

QUESTION 2: CURRENT CIRCUMSTANCES

How does knowing that God is faithful to forgive when you repent encourage you to confront areas of sin or guilt in your life?

_____

_____

_____

QUESTION 3: FUTURE PLANS - KNOWING THIS TRUTH

How can you cultivate a life of continual repentance and gratitude for God's forgiveness in your daily walk?

_____

_____

_____

A Prayer of Gratitude for the Gift of Repentance

Heavenly Father,

Thank You for granting me the gift of repentance and the forgiveness that flows from Your grace. I am humbled by Your mercy, which not only forgives but also transforms my heart to turn toward You. Help me to walk in humility and gratitude, continually seeking to align my life with Your will through repentance.

Teach me to reflect Your grace by forgiving others as You have forgiven me. May my life display the joy and freedom found in Your love and mercy.

In Jesus's Name,

Amen.

98. You Are a New Creation in Christ

Scripture

2 Corinthians 5:17 "Therefore, if anyone is in Christ, the new creation has come: The old has gone, the new is here." (NIV)

Romans 6:4 "We were therefore buried with him through baptism into death in order that, just as Christ was raised from the dead through the glory of the Father, we too may live a new life." (NIV)

Ephesians 4:24 "Put on the new self, created to be like God in true righteousness and holiness." (NIV)

Highlights

- **Transformational Truth:** At the moment of salvation, you become an new creation in Christ. You are a new creation, entirely transformed through the supernatural power of God.

- **Foundational Word:** "New creation" (Greek: *kainē ktisis*) refers to a profound transformation in a person's identity and nature, brought about by the regenerating work of the Holy Spirit.

- **Theological Insight**: Max Lucado explains, "God loves you just the way you are, but He refuses to leave you that way. He wants you to be just like Jesus."[99]

Grace Power-Up: New Creation in Christ

QUESTION 1: EXAMINING GOD'S CHARACTER

How would your life be different if you were still defined by your old self, unable to experience the transformation of being a new creation in Christ?

---

[99] Lucado, M. *Just Like Jesus: Learning to Have a Heart Like His.* Thomas Nelson, (1998). p. 3.

QUESTION 2: CURRENT CIRCUMSTANCES

How does knowing that you are a new creation inspire you to live a life that reflects God's love, hope, and purpose?

QUESTION 3: FUTURE PLANS - KNOWING THIS TRUTH

What steps can you take today to fully embrace your identity as a new creation and live in a way that demonstrates the power of Christ's transforming love to others?

A Prayer of Gratitude for Being a New Creation

Heavenly Father,

Thank You for making me a new creation in Christ. I am grateful that You have removed my old, sinful self and have given me a new identity, a new life in Christ, filled with purpose and hope. Thank You for the ongoing work of Your Spirit in my life, transforming me daily.

Help me to live in the fullness of this new life, reflecting Your love and grace in everything I do. Teach me to walk in righteousness and holiness, so my life glorifies You and inspires others to seek Your truth.

In Jesus's Name,
Amen.

99. You Are Brought Near to God

Scripture

Ephesians 2:13 "But now in Christ Jesus you who once were far away have been brought near by the blood of Christ." (NIV)

Highlights

- **Transformational Truth:** At the moment of salvation, you are brought near to God, experiencing a restored relationship and intimate fellowship through Christ's sacrifice.
- **Foundational Word:** "Brought near" (Greek: *engizō*) signifies being drawn into close proximity or relationship.
- **Theological Insight:** John Stott writes, "The blood of Christ bridges the infinite gap between a holy God and sinful humanity, bringing us into His presence."[100]

Grace Power-Up: Brought Near to God

QUESTION 1: EXAMINING GOD'S CHARACTER

How would your relationship with God and your life be impacted if Christ's sacrifice had **not** brought you near to Him, leaving you distant and separated?

_____

_____

_____

---

[100] John Stott, *The Cross of Christ* (Downers Grove, IL: InterVarsity Press, 1986), p. 173.

QUESTION 2: CURRENT CIRCUMSTANCES

How does knowing you have been brought near to God help you feel His presence and peace during times of struggle or uncertainty?

_____

_____

_____

QUESTION 3: FUTURE PLANS - KNOWING THIS TRUTH

How can you cultivate a deeper fellowship with God, embracing the intimacy made possible through Christ's sacrifice?

_____

_____

_____

A Prayer of Gratitude for Being Brought Near to God

Heavenly Father,

Thank You for bringing me near to You through the blood of Christ. I am overwhelmed by the grace that restored my relationship with You and allows me to experience Your presence intimately. Help me to cherish this closeness and seek You daily.

Teach me to live in the peace and joy of being near to You, trusting in Your love and guidance in every moment. May my life reflect the beauty of a restored relationship with You, drawing others to Your grace.

In Jesus's Name,
Amen.

100. You Are Given by the Father to the Son as a Love Gift

Scripture

Ephesians 1:4-5 "For he chose us in him before the creation of the world to be holy and blameless in his sight. In love he predestined us for adoption to sonship through Jesus Christ, in accordance with his pleasure and will." (NIV)

Highlights

- **Transformational Truth:** At the moment of salvation, you are given by the Father to the Son as a love gift, signifying the eternal unity and delight of the Godhead in redemption.
- **Foundational Word:** "Given" (Greek: *didōmi*) means to bestow or entrust, emphasizing the act of God the Father presenting believers to the Son.
- **Theological Insight:** John MacArthur states, "Believers are the Father's love gift to the Son, demonstrating the infinite love within the Trinity and the Son's perfect work of redemption."[101]

Grace Power-Up: Given by the Father to the Son as a Love Gift

QUESTION 1: EXAMINING GOD'S CHARACTER

How does understanding that God the Father has given you to the Son as a love gift reveal the depth of God's love and the unity of the Trinity?

---

[101] John MacArthur, *The MacArthur New Testament Commentary: John 12-21* (Chicago, IL: Moody Publishers, 2008), p. 87.

QUESTION 2: CURRENT CIRCUMSTANCES

How does knowing you are treasured as a love gift to Christ help you feel valued and secure in moments of doubt or struggle?

QUESTION 3: FUTURE PLANS - KNOWING THIS TRUTH

How can you live in a way that reflects the joy and gratitude of being a love gift from the Father to the Son, bringing glory to God?

A Prayer of Gratitude for Being Given as a Love Gift

Heavenly Father, thank You for making me a love gift to Your Son, a reflection of Your infinite love and grace. I am overwhelmed by the privilege of being entrusted to Christ, knowing He will never drive me away. Help me to live in the security and joy of this truth.

Teach me to glorify You in all I do, reflecting the love and unity of the Trinity. May my life be a testimony of gratitude and devotion, pointing others to Your incredible plan of redemption.

In Jesus's Name,

Amen.

How to Share Truths with Others

Romans Roadway for Salvation

1. Everyone Needs Salvation

Romans 3:23
"For all have sinned and fall short of the glory of God." (NIV)

Explanation: Every person has sinned and failed to meet God's perfect standard. We all need God's forgiveness.

2. The Consequences of Sin

Romans 6:23
"For the wages of sin is death, but the gift of God is eternal life in Christ Jesus our Lord." (NIV)

Explanation: Sin leads to eternal separation from God, but God offers the free gift of eternal life through Jesus.

3. God's Love and Provision

Romans 5:8
"But God demonstrates his own love for us in this: While we were still sinners, Christ died for us." (NIV)

Explanation: God loves us so much that He sent His Son, Jesus, to die for our sins, even when we didn't deserve it.

4. Salvation Through Faith

Romans 10:9-10
"If you declare with your mouth, 'Jesus is Lord,' and believe in your heart that God raised him from the dead, you will be saved. For it is with your heart that you believe and are justified, and it is with your mouth that you profess your faith and are saved." (NIV)

Explanation: Salvation comes through faith in Jesus—believing in His death and resurrection and confessing Him as Lord.

5. Assurance of Salvation

Romans 10:13
"For everyone who calls on the name of the Lord will be saved." (NIV)

Explanation: Anyone who sincerely asks Jesus for salvation will be saved—no matter their past.

6. Peace and a New Life in Christ

Romans 8:1
"Therefore, there is now no condemnation for those who are in Christ Jesus." (NIV)

Explanation: Once saved, you are free from guilt and condemnation, and you begin a new life in Christ.

What to Do Next

To respond to this message, you can pray something like this:

"Lord Jesus, I know that I do not deserve Your grace for the wrong things I have done and I need Your forgiveness. I trust and believe You died to pay for my sins and was buried and rose again and I thank You from allowing me this day to be a part of Your forever family, help me to live for You from this day forward. Thank You for giving me a new life in you. Amen."

Immediately: Share What Just Happened in Your Life!

Send us an email letting us know that you prayed this prayer. We will pray for you and provide additional materials to support you on your spiritual journey.

Your brother in Christ, joyfully serving.

Stephen Gowdy

Email: contact@brightideaspublishing.com

Become an Ambassador in 60 Seconds

You can share the life-saving truth of Jesus Christ using this simple 60-second tool!

Sharing your faith can be straightforward—and it can happen in just 60 seconds. Becoming a 60-Second Ambassador makes sharing your faith an enjoyable and impactful experience.

2 Corinthians 5:20 "We are therefore Christ's ambassadors, as though God were making his appeal through us. We implore you on Christ's behalf..." (NIV)

The Call to Be an Ambassador

The Lord wants to use you today as His ambassador, and the *One Minute Witness*[102] written by Tom Elie and modified slightly for this book, makes it easy to share your faith and make an eternal impact on someone's life. If you're willing to say "yes" to His prompting, here's how to get started.

THREE SIMPLE STEPS

1. **Pray**: Ask the Lord to open your heart and teach you how to be a 60-Second Ambassador.
2. **Learn**: Ask for courage to memorize 5 simple memory triggers.
3. **Act**: Ask the Lord to provide a kind and open person to share what you have learned.

The 5-Finger Framework

Each finger represents a key step in sharing your story. Use your hand as a reminder:

---

[102] Elie, Tom, & Oasis World Ministries. (n.d.). *One minute witness*. Champlin, MN: Oasis World Ministries. Retrieved from Oasisworldministries.org/one-minute-witness

THUMB: ASK TWO QUESTIONS

Starting with the thumb reminds us of asking for a "ride" when hitchhiking. It symbolizes asking two questions to open a conversation.

1. **"Can I ask you a question?"**
   Asking permission shows respect and opens the door for a conversation.

2. **"What is the best thing that has ever happened to you?"**
   Invite them to share their story. If they ask why you're asking, say: "Something amazing happened to me, and I wanted to know if others have experienced something like this."

Once they share, transition with:
"May I share the best thing that has ever happened to me?" or many times if you pause here ... people will beg for you to tell them "What is the best thing that has ever happened in your life?"

INDEX FINGER: TELL YOUR STORY (BEFORE CHRIST)

Your story begins with your life before knowing Christ. Use three adjectives or phrases to describe it:

Example: Lonely, frustrated, lacking purpose.
Write your own:

1. _____
2. _____
3. _____

MIDDLE FINGER: THE TURNING POINT

Everyone has a moment of spiritual awakening. Share yours.

Example: "I realized that Jesus loved me and died for my sins. When I understood this, I asked Him to forgive me and give me the gift of eternal life."

Write your turning point:

How did you hear about Jesus?

_____

Finish the sentence: "When I realized Jesus died for my sins, I..."

_____

RING FINGER: AFTER CHRIST

This is the positive transformation Christ has made in your life.

Example: Joy, purpose, assurance of eternal life.

Write three benefits Christ has brought into your life:

1. _____
2. _____
3. _____

PINKY: WITHOUT CHRIST

Reflect on what your life would be like without Jesus.

Example: "If I had never met Christ, my life would be empty and without hope."

Write your thoughts:

1. _____
2. _____
3. _____

Closing the Conversation

AFTER SHARING YOUR STORY, PLANT A SEED OF FAITH:

1. Thank them for listening.
2. Ask thought-provoking questions:
   - "If you died tonight, do you know for certain you would go to heaven?"
   - "How do you think someone gets to heaven?"

IF THEY'RE OPEN, SHARE HOW THEY CAN BE SAVED:

Romans 10:9-10 "If you declare with your mouth, 'Jesus is Lord,' and believe in your heart that God raised him from the dead, you will be saved. For it is with your heart that you believe and are justified, and it is with your mouth that you profess your faith and are saved." (NIV)

IF THEY ARE READY, ASK:

"With God's help, would you like to thank Him for His love and receive the free gift of eternal life today?"

A DAILY PRAYER

Dear Jesus, I am available. Please provide an opportunity to share my story today with someone kind and open to to talking with me. Amen.

TAKING IT FURTHER

After sharing your story:

Continue the conversation if they have questions.

Avoid debates or doctrinal discussions—focus on your personal story.

Remember: Your goal is to plant a seed of faith.

Closing Thoughts

Like the blind man in John 9:25 said, "I don't know much about this man who healed me. All I know is that I once was blind but now I see."

Have fun and share the Good News of Jesus Christ as an Ambassador in 60 seconds!

References, Resources, & Further Reading

Scriptures Referenced

Leviticus 17:11
John 10:28-29
Romans 3:24–25
Romans 3:25-26
Romans 5:1-5
Romans 5:8
Romans 5:10
Romans 6:4
Romans 6:14
Romans 6:23
Romans 7:4
Romans 7:6
Romans 8:1
Romans 8:15-16
Romans 8:26-27
Romans 8:29-30
Romans 8:33
Romans 8:34
Romans 8:37
Romans 8:38-39
Romans 10:9-10
Romans 12:1–2
Romans 12:19
1 Corinthians 1:2
1 Corinthians 3:8
1 Corinthians 3:9
1 Corinthians 3:11
1 Corinthians 3:13-15
1 Corinthians 3:16
1 Corinthians 6:11
1 Corinthians 6:19
1 Corinthians 6:20
1 Corinthians 7:23
1 Corinthians 9:24-27
1 Corinthians 12:12–13
1 Corinthians 13:4–7
1 Corinthians 15:3-4
1 Corinthians 15:57
2 Corinthians 1:3-4
2 Corinthians 1:21-22
2 Corinthians 3:3
2 Corinthians 3:5
2 Corinthians 3:11
2 Corinthians 3:18
2 Corinthians 5:17
2 Corinthians 5:18-19
2 Corinthians 5:20
2 Corinthians 6:1
2 Corinthians 7:10
2 Corinthians 12:9
Galatians 3:25
Galatians 4:4–5
Galatians 5:22-23
Galatians 6:14
Ephesians 1:3
Ephesians 1:4-5
Ephesians 1:6
Ephesians 1:7
Ephesians 1:11
Ephesians 1:13
Ephesians 2:4–5
Ephesians 2:6
Ephesians 2:8-9
Ephesians 2:18
Ephesians 2:19-20
Ephesians 3:3-6
Ephesians 3:8-9
Ephesians 3:11-12
Ephesians 4:2
Ephesians 4:20–24
Ephesians 5:8
Ephesians 5:32
Ephesians 6:12
Ephesians 6:17
Philippians 1:6
Philippians 1:29
Philippians 3:14
Philippians 3:20
Philippians 4:3
Philippians 4:4
Philippians 4:11-13
Colossians 1:12
Colossians 1:13
Colossians 1:14
Colossians 1:18
Colossians 1:22
Colossians 2:10
Colossians 2:11
Colossians 2:12
Colossians 2:14
Colossians 2:15
Colossians 3:1-2
Colossians 3:12–14
Colossians 3:24
1 Thessalonians 1:4
1 Thessalonians 1:6
1 Thessalonians 1:8
1 Thessalonians 5:17
1 Thessalonians 5:18
2 Thessalonians 1:3-4
2 Thessalonians 1:6-8
1 Timothy 1:15
2 Timothy 2:25
2 Timothy 3:12
2 Timothy 4:8
Titus 1:1
Titus 2:11-12
Titus 2:13
Hebrews 2:17
Hebrews 4:12
Hebrews 4:16
Hebrews 9:14
Hebrews 9:15
Hebrews 10:14
Hebrews 11:6
1 Peter 1:4
1 Peter 1:18
1 John 2:1
1 John 2:2
Revelation 13:8
Revelation 20:15
Revelation 21:27
Revelation 22:14

Resources

In developing this project, the author has drawn inspiration from a 2007-2008, year long conversation with Steve Imig in Duluth, Minnesota and the works of theologians who have explored the transformative events that occur at the moment of salvation. Notable contributions include:

- **Lewis Sperry Chafer**: *Systematic Theology. 33 distinct acts of divine grace*
- **Dann Spader and Dave Garda**: *33 Things That Happen at the Moment of Salvation* (Sonlife)
- **Grant C. Richison**: *Thirty-three Things Accomplished at Salvation*
- **Biblebelievers.com**: *38 Things That Happen When We Get Saved*
- **Paul Tautges**: *75 Astonishing Works that God Performs in Our Salvation*
- **Mark Matychuk:** *75 Things that happen at the moment of salvation*
- **Greater Grace Zimbabwe**: *95 Things That Happen at Salvation*
- **Tom Elie & Oasis World Ministries:** *One minute witness.*

The truths presented in this book are grounded solely in the Word of God, which serves as the ultimate authority for doctrine and theology. Supporting quotes from renowned theologians—and some less well-known—are included in the Highlights: **"Theological Insight"** to enrich your understanding of these truths. However, it should be noted that these theologians may not necessarily endorse every theological statement in this book, **though they should!** Their cited and referenced works serve as valuable insights and support for the specific truths they have previously addressed and believed in.

THE TRUTHS PRESENTED IN THIS BOOK ARE GROUNDED SOLELY IN THE WORD OF GOD, WHICH SERVES AS THE ULTIMATE AUTHORITY FOR DOCTRINE AND THEOLOGY.

While some theological concepts may appear similar to those of others, the nuanced variations in perspective and theology make each entry unique and valuable for inclusion in this work.

As you read, the author encourages you to approach each entry prayerfully, asking the Lord to reveal His truths through His Word and to guide you in applying these principles to your daily life. May this book be a tool to draw you closer to Him and inspire a life transformed by His grace and truth.

Special Thanks

To my mom, Mary Lou Gowdy*: a true living inspiration. Your daily reading of God's Word, applying it, and sharing it with others—unashamed yet with a tender and caring heart—has touched mine and so many other lives.

To my dad, Pastor "Uncle John" John A. Gowdy: if I become half the man you were, I will truly be a great man! You lived life "out loud," boldly, and with an infectious intensity that impacted everyone who met you. My Dear Old Dad (D.O.D.), I am grateful for your incredible legacy.

To my brothers, Jim, Tim, and Dan, and their spouses: Betsy, Grace* and Nancy; thank you for your encouragement and for standing boldly for Christ, serving in ways that honor the Lord. Special thanks to my sister-in-law Grace, whose editing help allowed me to find my written voice and convey what was truly on my heart.

To my children—Savannah*, Zechariah, Luke, and Joy—and their spouses: Lance, Joanna and Ryo and grandchildren Everette, Violet, Amelia, Malachi, Elias and Ezra: you inspire and encourage me daily. We love you all more than words can express.

To my business partner, Jason Christenson* and his wonderfully talented wife Brittany: thank you for the entrepreneurial adventures, your brilliant business insights, your encouragement, and your constant prayers.

To my dear brother in Christ, Steve Imig: this book's inspiration began with you in 2007–2008 as we prayed for our families, walked together, memorized Scripture, sang together, and encouraged each other by reciting the 100+ things that happen at the moment of salvation. Brother, I thank the Lord for you, and without your encouragement, this book would not exist.

To my kindred brother, Norm Cruthers: your encouragement, business acumen, and tenacity in holding me accountable were invaluable in seeing this project through.

To my dear friend Ken (and wife Kathy) Kemper: your example and inspiration gave me the confidence to believe I could write a book.

To my dear business-minded friend Rick Rush: who loves the Lord with all his heart. Thanks for your endless encouragement.

To my brothers-in-law Dwight Anderson*, Duane Anderson, and William Lange, and their spouses: Darlene, Lori, and Donna*: thank you for your dedication, lifelong examples and tireless work for the Lord.

To "my favorite" mother-in-law, Dorene Anderson: your passion for sharing the Gospel has made you one of the greatest soul-winners I know. The Romans

Roadway/Plan of Salvation included in this book are a testament to your desire to share God's truth with everyone.

To my aunts Joy Love Maslowski, Alice Faye Carter, and Margie (Anderson) Vinton: thank you for your love and encouragement throughout my life.

To Dr. Sam Vinton, Jr.: your life of faithful service to the Lord has been a shining example of wholehearted devotion.

To my dear friend and personal coach, Chris Cowling: your Holy Spirit-led sessions have guided this ministry to this point. Thank you for allowing the Lord to use you in this remarkable way.

To our Grand Rapids, Michigan Grace Bible Fellowship (GBF) Small Group Bible Study—Tim* and Beth* Postma, Charlie* and Jan* Young, Jon Young, and others: thank you for your fellowship, love, and support.

To our Young Marrieds "Deeper Truths" Bible Study group in Grand Rapids, Michigan: thank you for being my willing "test subjects" for the concepts in this book. Special thanks to Sean and Mary Martin, Robert and Natalie Kilgo, Kallyn and Joanna Gowdy, Haley and Loren Forbes, and occasional visitors like Franz and Anna Craesmeyer.

To my dear friends Rick and Kim Pilieci: your lives exemplify wholehearted service to the Lord.

To my co-workers at Grace Christian University: working alongside you in ministry was a joy. Special thanks to Ami and Bryan Walker, Austin and Autumn Olson, Becca and Chip Schaffran, Becky Karsten, Bev Wallace, Brian and Pam Sherstad, Colton Wolfe, Cory Jamison, Dave Greydanus, Dave and Linda Holton, David Turner, Dawn Rodgers, Doug and Lynne Vrisman, Ellie Glass, Emily and Jason Lazor, Emilee Prins, Erin and Matt Hubner, Hilary and Kyle and Hilary Vegh, Jeff Brodrick, Jim and Emily Gamble, Julie and Scott Priolo, Kyle and Lindsay Bohl, Mat and Michelle Loverin, Matt De Young, Nat Mercer, Scott and Luanne Shaw, Sherea Lacy, Ron and Statia Merrihew, Todd Coats, Tyler and Susan Bauer, Tim and Sue Rumley, and Zak Sorenson.

To Pastor Caleb Befus and his wife Mary: your unwavering love for the Lord and your genuine encouragement have been a tremendous example of balancing ministry, family, and personal devotion to God's Word.

To my "Prayer Warriors": your faithful intercession has been a lifeline in this ministry. Thank you to Ab and Margaret Lee, Adam Javed, Al and Cheryl Larson, Al Wolf, Alejandro and Loriana Gonzalez, Alison Taylor, Amiee Johnson, Andy and Sue Hollenbeck, Anna Lange*, Anthony and Pamela Beaulieu, Barb Gowdy, Barb Molitoris, Ben Lange, Bill and Phyl Krombeen, Bill Lettinga, Bill Marvin, Bill Noller, Bill Rigg, Billy Doran, Bob and Joyce Storms, Bryan Gordon, Caleb Lange, and Cameron and Lindsay Townley, Carolyn Burleson, Chris Tamara and Hankins, Craig Baker, Craig and Sherry Hoppen, Dale and Dawn Day, Dale and Marcy Dugan, Darla Adams, Dan and Nancy Spooner, Dan and Willamena

Myers, Dan* and Jennifer* Sidebottom (thanks for the hours and hours of editing assistance), Dave Albright, Dave and Lisa Cannon, Dave and Joan Velting, Dave and Darla Chinn, Dave and Jenny Green, Dave and Lisa Kepner, David Noebel, Dean DeGraff, Dennis and Faith Smith, Drew and Dionna Gustafson, Dominic Siciliano, Don and Rindy Koukal, Don and Sandy Medema, Don and Sandy Tenhove*, Doug and Karen Helmer, Doug Waltz, Edward Stratton, Frank and Mary Shemonek, Gary Bailey, Gary and Sherrie Leyendecker, Glen and Lisa Beauchamp, Glenn Rhodes, Greg and Kendra Adams, Greg and Nannette Bunch, Greg and Alison Reuter, Gretchen Johnson, Jack and Bea Retzer, Jack and Jean Capen, Jack and Kathy Taylor, Jake Miedema, Jared and Abby Lowder, Jerry Hop, Jim and Joy Albers, Jim Anton, Jim Bob and Joan Roberts, Jim and Denise Carlson, Jim and Theresa Kemp, Jim and April Loppnow, Jim Stringham, Jim and Jenni McGillicuddy, Jim Vandergesson, Jim and Kathy Molenkamp, Jimmy and Carolyn Moore, Joe Albers, Joe and Cheryl Matthis, Joe Vogan, John and Becky Christenson, John Kelly, John and Melinda Lowder, Jon Michael and Olivia Clark, Joyce Webb, Kay Postma, Ken Filippini, Keoante Blackamore, Kerry Malakosky, Kerry Quam, Kevin and Luann Velting, Kim Velting, Kris Anderson, Lisa Menefee, Lowell and Char Anderson, Luke and Dolly Hunt, Marcelo and Daniella De Souza, Mark Love, Mark and Elizabeth Soy, Matt and Sharon Amundson, Michael Poulsen, Michelle Burleson, Mick Volkhardt, Mike Bradley, Mike and Donna Dunn, Mike Zuverink, Nathan and Brenda Tuttle, Paul and Elayn Marcus, Paula Lenger, Phillip and Brenda Cereghino, Randy Zanbergen, Ray and Liz Marcucci, Rich* and Laura Wiersma, Rob and Amy Renberg, Rob Sunman, Robert and Linda Nix, Rod Cotz, Roger Sonneveldt, Russ Kopp, Ruth Harlan, Ryan Pylman, Scott Albers, Scott and Donna Velting, Shari Huber, Shawn Huber, Sherwood Sage, Spencer and Laura Kilgore, Steve and Debbie Blackwell, Steve and Diane Carpenter, Steve and Joy Hartman, Steve and Annette Postma, Steve and Barb Sherman, Steve Vanderwall, Steve Wendt, Susie Magnusen, Terry Yoder, Tim and Lori Board, Tim and Beth Osterland, Tim Goeglien, Tom Brew, Tom and Leslie Brookhouse, Troy and Tiffany Sergey, Truman and Pat Wigen, Wade and Beth Rustin, Wally and Beth Johnson, Wayne and Karen Matychuk, and so many others.

To our "Attic Dwellers," Chloe Pouliot and Carolann Bloom: your time with us was a blessing, and your presence in our lives during that season was impactful.

To my lovely wife, Darlene Gowdy* (who humbly asked to be listed last), whose gentle hand of love and guidance is a gift beyond what I deserve. I love you deeply and treasure "Doing Life Together."

* - Individuals with significant editing assistance.

Author's Note

As I reflect on the journey of writing this book, I am struck by how deeply personal and transformative the process has been. Frankly, writing my first book has been extremely difficult, humbling, and filled with moments of self-doubt and self-discovery. Initially, the structure of the book leaned toward an academic approach, meticulously naming each theological concept. However, at the suggestion of a dear friend, I shifted to framing these truths in the second person, crafting "You Statements" that directly speak to the reader. This change was made late in the writing process, and as I reread each article in this new light, I found myself pausing to take in the profound realities of what each statement represented.

AS I CONTEMPLATED EACH ARTICLE, IT BROUGHT ME TO TEARS. IT IS OVERWHELMING TO THINK ABOUT ALL THAT THE LORD HAS DONE FOR ME ON THE CROSS AND WHAT I RECEIVED AT THE MOMENT OF SALVATION.

Those moments of reflection were powerful. As I contemplated each article, it brought me to tears. It is overwhelming to think about all that the Lord has done for me on the Cross and what I received at the moment of salvation. To say "Wow!" feels like an understatement. The depth of God's grace, love, and provision left me in awe, and I pray that this book helps you experience the same wonder I feel.

I CHALLENGE YOU TO DISCOVER A FEW TRANSFORMATIVE TRUTHS FROM GOD'S WORD THAT MAY HAVE BEEN OVERLOOKED IN THIS BOOK. I'M CONFIDENT THERE COULD BE ANOTHER 100 WAITING TO BE FOUND. LET ME KNOW—PERHAPS WE CAN COLLABORATE ON A SECOND EDITION TOGETHER! STEPHEN GOWDY

During this process, I also revisited the list of articles to ensure each concept was as impactful and distinct as possible. With a goal to keep the number of articles to 100, I found that a number articles needed to be replaced to strengthen the overall message and avoid redundancy. Here are a few:

1. "You Are Pardoned from Sin's Penalty"

Overlaps significantly with "Your Sins Are Forgiven Forever" and "Christ Paid the Penalty for Your Sin."

2. "Granted Access to God's Kingdom"

Themes of access and belonging to God's kingdom are well-addressed in "You Are a Citizen of Heaven."

3. "You Have the Power to Be Patient in Relationships"

Overlaps with relational themes like "You Have the Power to Love Fully" and "You Can Cultivate an Unoffendable Heart."

4. "You Are Circumcised in Christ"

While significant, the concept may feel less immediately relevant and requires a significant explanation of biblical history compared to other truths. It also overlaps with "You Are Made Perfect in Christ" and "You Are Complete in Him."

5. "You Have Entered the Kingdom of His Son"

While this topic is important, its theological concept overlaps with other articles addressing the believer's new identity and position, such as: "You Are a Citizen of Heaven" and "You Have Been Added to the Body of Believers."

Each article was carefully chosen to enhance the clarity and breadth of the truths presented. My hope is that as you read these "You Statements," you will pause, reflect, and be moved by the enormity of what Christ has done for you. This book is not just a collection of theological concepts; it is a celebration of God's unending love and grace. May these truths sink deep into your heart and inspire you to live in the fullness of all you have in Him.

6. "You are a Minister of the The New Covenant"

2 Corinthians 3:6

7. "You have Confidence thought Christ before God"

2 Corinthians 3:4

8. "You were given a Spirit of power, love and self-discipline."

2 Timothy1:7

Why "Game Changer?"

I've been asked about the title *Game Changer* and how I came up with it. Let me share a few thoughts to provide some context.

In this book, the term *Game Changer* symbolizes the profound and transformative impact that faith in Jesus Christ has on an individual's life.

1. **Life-Altering Moment of Salvation**
   The title emphasizes that accepting Christ as Savior is not just a minor adjustment but a radical shift. It's a complete redefinition of identity, purpose, and destiny. Faith in Jesus changes everything the moment someone believes—it's truly a *game changer*.

2. **Core Truths That Transform**
   The 100 truths presented in this book highlight specific ways that faith reshapes a person's life. These truths act as building blocks for spiritual maturity, offering practical and theological insights that are "game changers" for understanding God's grace, love, and purpose.

3. **A Guide to a New Way of Living**
   This book is designed to encourage readers to reflect, pray, and apply these truths to their daily lives. Actively engaging with God's Word through these principles can lead to life-changing realizations about living for God.

4. **Hope and Empowerment**
   The title reflects the hope and empowerment believers receive upon salvation—a shift from spiritual death to life, from being lost to being found, and from self-reliance to trusting God's grace.

5. **A Call to Action**
   Game Changer serves as an invitation to embrace these truths fully and allow them to revolutionize your life. It's a call to see faith as dynamic and powerful, capable of transforming not just your life but also the lives of others.

The title encapsulates the theme of transformation at the heart of this book: how God's truths reshape our lives at the moment of salvation and continues to impact us as we grow in Christ.

A Personal Reflection

The inspiration for this title came from two personal experiences.

First, during one of my past business ventures, the Chief Information Officer (CIO) of one of the world's largest big-box electronic retailers visited my company for a week. His goal was to determine if my growing company was working on what he referred to as a "disruptive technology."

He explained that his company sold hundreds of thousands of wireless routers each month—sometimes more than 800,000 in a single month. While the routers themselves had slim profit margins, they drove significant profit through high margin peripheral equipment like cabling. He was concerned that the work we were doing with WiMAX in collaboration with Intel and other tech companies could disrupt this revenue stream.

That conversation profoundly impacted me. It underscored how certain innovations—disruptive technologies—can change the game entirely, reshaping industries and altering trajectories. It was a game changer. Of course, calling this book *Disruptive Technology: 100 Truths That Transform Your Life* didn't seem as catchy!

Second, I explained the concept to my mother-in-law using a football analogy. Imagine a key football player is injured, and a replacement steps in and plays so phenomenally well that he turned the game around for their team. At the end of the game, the coach awarded the replacement player the "game ball", recognizing his pivotal role. That player is what I would call a real "Game Changer."

A new life in Christ is exactly that—a transformative power that turns your life around and reshapes your eternal destiny.

References (Sorted by Theologian)

Batterson, Mark, *Nostalgia for God*. [Blog post]. Retrieved from https://www.markbatterson.com/nostalgia-for-god/ (2020, August 5).
Baker, Charles F., *Understanding God's Sovereignty: Trusting His Justice and Timing* (Grand Rapids, MI: Grace Bible Press, 1965), p. 132.
Baker, Charles F., *A Dispensational Theology* (Grand Rapids, MI: Grace Bible College Publications, 1971), p. 348.
Baker, Charles F., *A Dispensational Theology* (Grand Rapids, MI: Grace Bible College Publications, 1971), p. 421.
Bruce, F.F., *The Epistle to the Philippians* (Grand Rapids, MI: Eerdmans, 1983), p. 104.
Bruce, F.F., *The Epistles to the Colossians, to Philemon, and to the Ephesians* (Grand Rapids, MI: Eerdmans, 1984), p. 57.
Bultema, Harry, *Living by Grace: God's Provision for Every Need* (Grand Rapids, MI: Kregel Publications, 1954), p. 112.
Calvin, John, *Institutes of the Christian Religion*, Book III, Chapter 3, Section 9 (Edinburgh: Calvin Translation Society, 1845).
Calvin, John, *Institutes of the Christian Religion*, Book III, Chapter 20, Section 3 (Edinburgh: Calvin Translation Society, 1845).
Calvin, John, *Commentary on the Epistles of Paul the Apostle to the Philippians, Colossians, and Thessalonians* (Edinburgh: Calvin Translation Society, 1851), commentary on Colossians 2:11.
Calvin, John, *Institutes of the Christian Religion*, Book III, Chapter 2, Section 11 (Edinburgh: Calvin Translation Society, 1845).
Calvin, John, *Institutes of the Christian Religion*, Book III, Chapter 11, Section 2 (Edinburgh: Calvin Translation Society, 1845).
Calvin, John, *Institutes of the Christian Religion*, Book III, Chapter 11, Section 6 (Edinburgh: Calvin Translation Society, 1845).
Calvin, John, *Institutes of the Christian Religion*, Book III, Chapter 6, Section 3 (Edinburgh: Calvin Translation Society, 1845).
Elie, Tom, & Oasis World Ministries. *One Minute Witness*. Champlin, MN: Oasis World Ministries. Retrieved from Oasisworldministries.org/one-minute-witness.
Evans, Tony, *Victory in Spiritual Warfare: Outfitting Yourself for the Battle*. Harvest House Publishers, (2011). p. 42.
Gowdy, John, *Grace in Action: Living Out Christ's Redemption Daily* (Green Valley, AZ: Redemption Press, 2020), p. 112.
Gowdy, John, *Grace Unveiled: Understanding the Gift of Salvation* (Green Valley, AZ: Redemption Press, 2021), p. 76.

Gowdy, John, *Eternal Perspective: Living for What Matters Most* (Green Valley, AZ: Redemption Press, 2022), p. 89.

Gowdy, John, *Grace in Action: Living with an Un-offendable Heart* (Green Valley, AZ: Redemption Press, 2022), p. 78.

Graham, Billy, *The Holy Spirit: Activating God's Power in Your Life* (Nashville, TN: Thomas Nelson, 1978), p. 104.

Graham, Billy, *New Heaven, New Earth*. Billy Graham Evangelistic Association. (2011, May 9). Retrieved from https://billygraham.org/devotion/new-heaven-new-earth/

Henry, Matthew, *Matthew Henry's Commentary on the Whole Bible*, commentary on Hebrews 9:15.

Henry, Matthew, *Matthew Henry's Commentary on the Whole Bible*, commentary on 1 Peter 1:4.

Hodge, Charles, *Systematic Theology*, Vol. 3 (New York: Scribner, Armstrong & Co., 1873), p. 593.

Hodge, Charles, *Systematic Theology*, Vol. 2 (New York: Scribner, Armstrong & Co., 1873), p. 471.

Ingram, Chip, *God: As He Longs for You to See Him* (Grand Rapids, MI: Baker Books, 2004), p. 87.

Kemper, Ken, *Living in Christ: Reflections on Discipleship and Relationship* (Grand Rapids, MI: Grace Publications, 2018), p. 89.

Kemper, Ken, *Ambassadors of Grace: Living Out Reconciliation in a Broken World* (Grand Rapids, MI: Grace Publications, 2019), p. 124.

Kemper, Ken, *Equipped by the Word: Living with Power and Protection* (Grand Rapids, MI: Grace Publications, 2020), p. 115.

Kemper, Ken, *Living Grace: Extending Forgiveness and Reflecting Christ* (Grand Rapids, MI: Grace Publications, 2020), p. 112.

Keller, Timothy, *Encounters with Jesus: Unexpected Answers to Life's Biggest Questions*. Dutton, 2013, p. 102.

Kendall, R.T., (1998). *The Anointing: Yesterday, Today, and Tomorrow*. Charisma House, p. 63.

Lucado, Max, *Just Like Jesus: Learning to Have a Heart Like His*. Thomas Nelson, (1998). p. 3.

Luther, Martin, *Commentary on Galatians 1* (Grand Rapids: Kregel Publications, 1979), p. 20.

Luther, Martin, *Commentary on Galatians* (1535), translated by Erasmus Middleton, p. 85.

Lutzer, Erwin W., *The Cross in the Shadow of the Crescent* (Eugene, OR: Harvest House Publishers, 2013), p. 132.

Lutzer, Erwin W., *The Cross in the Shadow of the Crescent* (Eugene, OR: Harvest House Publishers, 2013), p. 78.

Lutzer, Erwin W., The Vanishing Power of Death: Conquering Sin and Claiming Victory in Christ (Chicago, IL: Moody Publishers, 2004), p. 132.

MacArthur, John, *The Gospel According to Jesus* (Grand Rapids, MI: Zondervan, 1988), p. 203.

MacArthur, John, *The MacArthur Study Bible* (Nashville, TN: Thomas Nelson, 1997), commentary on Hebrews 10:1-10.
MacArthur, John, *The Believer's Life in Christ: Ephesians* (Chicago, IL: Moody Press, 1986), p. 37.
MacArthur, John, *The Gospel According to Jesus: What Does Jesus Mean When He Says 'Follow Me'?* (Grand Rapids, MI: Zondervan, 1994), p. 104.
MacArthur, John, *The MacArthur New Testament Commentary: Ephesians* (Chicago, IL: Moody Publishers, 1986), p. 98.
MacArthur, John, *The MacArthur New Testament Commentary: Colossians and Philemon* (Chicago, IL: Moody Publishers, 1992), p. 45.
MacArthur, John, *The MacArthur New Testament Commentary: John 12-21* (Chicago, IL: Moody Publishers, 2008), p. 87.
MacArthur, John, *The MacArthur New Testament Commentary: Romans 1-8* (Chicago, IL: Moody Publishers, 1991), p. 327.
MacArthur, John, *The MacArthur New Testament Commentary: Colossians and Philemon* (Chicago, IL: Moody Publishers, 1992), p. 104.
MacArthur, John, *The MacArthur New Testament Commentary: Hebrews* (Chicago, IL: Moody Publishers, 1983), p. 112.
MacArthur, John, *The MacArthur New Testament Commentary: Romans 9-16* (Chicago, IL: Moody Publishers, 1994), p. 352.
MacArthur, John, *The MacArthur New Testament Commentary: Hebrews* (Chicago, IL: Moody Publishers, 1983), p. 409.
MacArthur, John, *The MacArthur New Testament Commentary: 1 & 2 Thessalonians* (Chicago, IL: Moody Publishers, 2002), p. 28.
MacArthur, John, *The MacArthur New Testament Commentary: Philippians* (Chicago, IL: Moody Publishers, 2001), p. 47.
MacArthur, John, *The MacArthur New Testament Commentary: 2 Corinthians* (Chicago, IL: Moody Publishers, 2003), p. 236.
MacArthur, John, *The MacArthur New Testament Commentary: Ephesians* (Chicago, IL: Moody Publishers, 1986), p. 304.
MacArthur, John, *The MacArthur New Testament Commentary: 1 Corinthians* (Chicago, IL: Moody Publishers, 1984), p. 295.
MacArthur, John, *The MacArthur New Testament Commentary: Philippians* (Chicago, IL: Moody Publishers, 2001), p. 166.
MacArthur, John, *Alone with God: Rediscovering the Power and Passion of Prayer* (Colorado Springs, CO: David C. Cook, 1995), p. 42.
Menikoff, Aaron, *Adoption: The Heart of the Gospel. In Character Matters: Shepherding in the Fruit of the Spirit.* (Wheaton, IL: Crossway. 2019), p. 143
Moody, D.L., *Secret Power: The Secret of Success in Christian Life and Work* (Chicago, IL: Fleming H. Revell Company, 1881), p. 49.
Moody, D.L., *The Overcoming Life* (Chicago, IL: Fleming H. Revell Company, 1896), p. 87.
Owen, John, *The Works of John Owen, Vol. 6: The Doctrine of the Saints' Perseverance Explained and Confirmed* (Edinburgh: Banner of Truth Trust, 1967), p. 305.
Owen, John, *The works of John Owen, Volume 6. Edinburgh:* Johnstone and Hunter. (1850). p. 352.

Packer, J.I., *Knowing God* (Downers Grove, IL: InterVarsity Press, 1973), p. 207.
Packer, J.I., *Knowing God* (Downers Grove, IL: InterVarsity Press, 1973), p. 207.
Piper, John, *Desiring God: Meditations of a Christian Hedonist* (Colorado Springs, CO: Multnomah, 2003), p. 54.
Piper, John, *The Future of Justification: A Response to N.T. Wright* (Wheaton, IL: Crossway Books, 2007), p. 64.
Piper, John, *Future Grace: The Purifying Power of the Promises of God* (Colorado Springs, CO: Multnomah, 1995), p. 234.
Piper, John, *Desiring God: Meditations of a Christian Hedonist* (Colorado Springs, CO: Multnomah, 2003), p. 33.
Piper, John, *Let the Nations Be Glad: The Supremacy of God in Missions* (Grand Rapids, MI: Baker Academic, 2003), p. 65.
Sproul, R.C., *Chosen by God* (Wheaton, IL: Tyndale House Publishers, 1986), p. 150.
Sproul, R.C., *What Is the Kingdom of God?* (Sanford, FL: Reformation Trust, 2017), p. 42.
Spurgeon, Charles, *All of Grace* (London: Passmore and Alabaster, 1886), p. 67.
Spurgeon, Charles, *Morning and Evening* (London: Passmore and Alabaster, 1865), entry for Romans 5:10.
Spurgeon, Charles, *Metropolitan Tabernacle Pulpit, Vol. 25, Sermon No. 1497: The Ministry of Reconciliation* (London: Passmore and Alabaster, 1879), p. 314.
Spurgeon, Charles, *Metropolitan Tabernacle Pulpit, Vol. 34, Sermon No. 2004: The Reward of the Righteous* (London: Passmore and Alabaster, 1888), p. 428.
Spurgeon, Charles, *Metropolitan Tabernacle Pulpit, Vol. 36, Sermon No. 2132: Faith's Reward* (London: Passmore and Alabaster, 1890), p. 467.
Spurgeon, Charles, *Metropolitan Tabernacle Pulpit, Vol. 27, Sermon No. 1605: Trust in God Alone* (London: Passmore and Alabaster, 1881), p. 362.
Spurgeon, Charles, *Metropolitan Tabernacle Pulpit, Vol. 22, Sermon No. 1287: The Joy of the Lord in Suffering* (London: Passmore and Alabaster, 1876), p. 497.
Spurgeon, Charles, *Metropolitan Tabernacle Pulpit, Vol. 19, Sermon No. 1127: The Inheritance of the Saints* (London: Passmore and Alabaster, 1873), p. 354.
Spurgeon, Charles, *Metropolitan Tabernacle Pulpit, Vol. 31, Sermon No. 1848: The Throne of Grace* (London: Passmore and Alabaster, 1885), p. 387.
Spurgeon, Charles, *Metropolitan Tabernacle Pulpit, Vol. 25, Sermon No. 1487: The Simplicity and Power of the Gospel* (London: Passmore and Alabaster, 1879), p. 246.
Spurgeon, Charles, *Metropolitan Tabernacle Pulpit, Vol. 7, Sermon No. 402: The Unmerited Love of God* (London: Passmore and Alabaster, 1861), p. 263.
Spurgeon, Charles, *Morning and Evening* (London: Passmore and Alabaster, 1866), devotional entry on 1 John 2:1.
Spurgeon, Charles, *Metropolitan Tabernacle Pulpit, Vol. 25, Sermon No. 1463: The Temple of the Living God* (London: Passmore and Alabaster, 1879), p. 314.
Stam, C.R., *Things That Differ: The Fundamentals of Dispensationalism* (Germantown, WI: Berean Bible Society, 1951), p. 157.
Stam, C.R., *True Spiritual Worship: Living a Life of Grace* (Grand Rapids, MI: Berean Bible Society, 1959), p. 142.
Stott, John, *The Message of 2 Corinthians: Power in Weakness* (Downers Grove, IL:

InterVarsity Press, 1988), p. 93.

Stott, John, *The Cross of Christ* (Downers Grove, IL: IVP Books, 1986), p. 162.

Stott, John, *The Message of 1 Corinthians: Life in the Local Church* (Downers Grove, IL: InterVarsity Press, 1985), p. 222.

Stott, John, *The Cross of Christ* (Downers Grove, IL: InterVarsity Press, 1986), p. 199.

Stott, John, *The Cross of Christ* (Downers Grove, IL: InterVarsity Press, 1986), p. 173.

Stott, John, *The Message of Ephesians: God's New Society* (Downers Grove, IL: InterVarsity Press, 1979), p. 198.

Stott, John, *The Message of Ephesians: God's New Society* (Downers Grove, IL: InterVarsity Press, 1979), p. 31.

Stott, John, *The Message of Galatians: Only One Way* (Downers Grove, IL: InterVarsity Press, 1968), p. 152.

Stott, John, *The Message of 1 Timothy and Titus: The Life of the Local Church* (Downers Grove, IL: InterVarsity Press, 1996), p. 102.

Swindoll, Charles R., *The Grace Awakening* (Dallas, TX: Word Publishing, 1990), p. 112.

Swindoll, Charles R., *Strengthening Your Grip: How to Be Grounded in a Chaotic World* (Nashville, TN: Thomas Nelson, 2011), p. 48.

Tozer, A.W., *The Purpose of Man: Designed to Worship* (Ventura, CA: Regal Books, 2009), p. 174.

Tozer, A.W., *The Pursuit of God* (Camp Hill, PA: Christian Publications, 1948), p. 121.

Vinton, Sam Jr., *Eternal Security: Resting in God's Faithfulness* (Grand Rapids, MI: Grace Publications, 2008), p. 134.

Vinton, Sam Jr., *The Mystery of Christ and the Church* (Grand Rapids, MI: Grace Publications, 2008), p. 145.

Vinton, Sam Jr., *The Church: God's Masterpiece of Grace* (Grand Rapids, MI: Grace Publications, 2005), p. 72.

Vinton, Sam Jr., *Set Free by Grace: Living in the Power of the Spirit* (Grand Rapids, MI: Grace Publications, 2009), p. 92.

Vinton, Sam Jr., *The Heart of the Gospel: God's Love and Grace* Revealed (Grand Rapids, MI: Grace Publications, 2015), p. 64.

Vinton, Sam Jr., *The Precious Blood: Redemption and Reconciliation Through Christ* (Grand Rapids, MI: Grace Publications, 2006), p. 88.

About the Author

Stephen C. Gowdy, a pastor and lifelong entrepreneur, brings a passion for Christ-centered service to everything he does. Together with his wife of 40 years, they prayerfully hope *Game Changer: 100 Truths That Transform Your Life the Moment You Believe* will inspire your faith journey and deepen your relationship with Christ.

Stephen's journey includes decades of leadership in education and ministry, including serving for the past 7 years as a University Administrator and Vice President of Advancement at a West Michigan Christian university, where he championed opportunities for transformative, faith-based education. His heart for outreach began more than 45 years ago at Bible youth camps around the nation and continues efforts to make biblical collegiate education accessible to underserved communities.

An ordained minister of the Gospel of Jesus Christ by the Grace Gospel Fellowship, Stephen holds a Religious Education Degree from Grace Christian

University. His calling is to help others encounter God's truth and experience the life-changing power of biblical education and transformational relationships.

Happily married to his wife Darlene of 40 years (Darlene says 38 have been great), they are proud parents of four and grandparents of six.

Stephen and Darlene joyfully pray that as you explore God's Word, you find salvation, peace, and freedom through Jesus Christ alone.

Joyfully Serving,

Stephen

Before You Go

PLEASE REVIEW!

If you enjoyed *Game Changer: 100 Truths That Transform Your Life the Moment You Believe*, would you consider leaving feedback on amazon.com, your local store, or your bookseller of choice? I would greatly appreciate it!

These reviews also make this book more visible to those who otherwise might not discover it. Everyone seems to request reviews these days, but be assured your thoughts and comments will be valued and appreciated.

WANT TO BUY IN BULK OR PURCHASE ADDITIONAL COPIES FOR YOUR CHURCH, ORGANIZATION, OR BIBLE STUDY GROUP?

WOULD YOU LIKE ASSISTANCE PUBLISHING YOUR OWN BOOK? WE COULD HELP!

BRIGHT IDEAS PUBLISHING

Green Valley | Arizona | USA

BrightIdeasPublishing.com

Please email contact@BrightIdeasPublishing.com

www.ingramcontent.com/pod-product-compliance
Lightning Source LLC
LaVergne TN
LVHW020926090426
835512LV00020B/3217